THE BEST OF
PRIVATE EYE
1995

D1421714

ALSO AVAILABLE FROM PRIVATE EYE • CORGI

THE PRIVATE EYE BOOK OF CRAIG BROWN PARODIES

In this brand new collection of parodies, Craig Brown extends a welcoming claw to Margaret Thatcher, Newman and Baddiel, Martin Amis, Linda McCartney and Michael Winner, among many others.
£4.99

THE 4TH & FINAL SECRET DIARY OF JOHN MAJOR

They said there would never be another instalment of John Major's world famous Secret Diary – but they were in no small measure wrong. Here in the fourth and final diary the Prime Minister is left alone, or right alone, depending on who he is talking to.
£4.99

SON OF YOBS

Another collection of Yobs and other cartoons by Tony Husband in this sequel to the best-selling 'YOBS'.
£3.99

Published in Great Britain by
Private Eye Productions Ltd, 6 Carlisle Street, London W1V 5RG
in association with Corgi Books

©1995 Pressdram Ltd.
ISBN 0 552 14402 9
Cover image by Sightlines
Designed by Bridget Tisdall
Printed in England by Ebenezer Baylis & Son Ltd, Worcester

Corgi Books are published by Transworld Publishers Ltd 61–63 Uxbridge Road, Ealing, London W5 5SA
in Australia by Transworld Publishers (Australia) Pty, Ltd 15–23 Helles Avenue, Moorebank, NSW 2170
and in New Zealand by Transworld Publishers (N.Z.) Ltd 3 William Pickering Drive, Albany, Auckland.
2 4 6 8 10 9 7 5 3 1

THE BEST OF PRIVATE EYE 1995

MAGIC PRIVATE EYE

A New Way of Looking at the World

Edited by Ian Hislop

PRIVATE EYE • CORGI

MAGIC EYE CABINET
STARE AT THIS IMAGE OF DEADBEATS UNTIL YOU BEHOLD A MAGICAL NEW TEAM OF WINNERS!

Interest rate rise surprises Liz Hurley

by Our Hurley Correspondent LUNCHTIME O'GLE

THE ACTRESS Liz Hurley, girlfriend of Hugh Grant, the star of the smash hit British comedy *Four Weddings and a Funeral*, was said yesterday to have had "no idea that the Chancellor was about to put ½% on interest rates".

Friends of the actress say that the interest rate rise was not something Liz had ever imagined for the autumn. A close colleague told the Hurleygraph: "Liz feels that, with 3% growth and a 2% inflation rate, the Chancellor had very little room to manoeuvre."

Cor!

No comment from Hurley on two-speed Europe

by Our Assistant Hurley Correspondent QUENTIN LECH

THE ACTRESS Elizabeth Hurley, girlfriend of Hugh Grant, the star of the smash hit British comedy *Four Weddings and a Funeral*, was said last night to be "keeping a close eye" on the EC row over Franco-German plans for a "hard-core, two-tier Europe".

Said a close friend: "Look, she's an actress, for God's sake. Can you stop ringing me up?"

Rail strike spells chaos for Hurley

by Our Deputy Hurley Correspondent CHARLES MORE-HURLEY-PLEASE

THE FAILURE of Railtrack and the RMT to reach agreement and end the long-running signalmen's dispute has proved disastrous for top actress Elizabeth Hurley, girlfriend of Hugh Grant, the star of the smash hit British comedy *Four Weddings and a Funeral*.

"Liz has been unable to travel by train on strike days," says a close friend, "except of course when there is a service still running. She has been obliged to travel by car on some days, I gather, which is very inconvenient because of parking."

Railtrack boss Bob Reid yesterday apologised to customers, including Liz Hurley, for the continuing disruption.

ON OTHER PAGES

MATT

"Man bites dog's not news – dog doesn't bite Liz Hurley, now that's news!"

Phworr!!

Blimey!

THE ARCHERS

An Everyday Story of Share-Dealing Folk

(Theme tune fades to sound of church clock striking three. Tinkle of teacups on vicarage lawn. There is the sound of a distant fax machine.)

Jeff Archer: You're not expecting anything, are you, Mary?

Mary Archer: Nothing except the timing of the announcement on the takeover bid for Anglia.

Jeff: Oh, only that. I've got to go into the house to write a new novel. I'll fetch it for you.

Mary: If it's for me, you mustn't read it. It's highly confidential.

(Sound of rustling paper)

Jeff *(to self)*: Cripes, this is hot stuff. *(Aloud)* It's for me, dear. It's from my publishers. They've finished writing my new book.

(Cut to saloon bar of the Grantchester Arms)

Landlord: Hello, Jeff. You're in early today, me old beauty.

Archer: Can I use your phone, Jim? Ours is… er… temporarily out of order.

Landlord: Certainly. Help yourself, squire. Got a hot tip, have you?

Archer: Something like that. *(Laughs triumphantly)*

(Sound of dialling)

Yokel: Have you filled in your set-aside yet, Walter?

2nd Yokel: Why, of course oi 'ave. Oi knows the old rhyme:
"No subsidies for set-aside
Unless you've applied by Lammas-tide."

(Laughter. Chink of glasses)

3rd Yokel: Is it barley again this year, Seth?

4th Yokel: No, we went there last year. This year it's Bangkok.

(Cut back to Archer on telephone)

Archer: That's right, Charlie, two hundred and fifty thou' on the number three account, and I want it in the usual name… *(fades)*

Jeff Archer *(returning home)*: Hello, darling. I didn't read that fax, honest. And it wasn't for you, anyway…

(Closing music)

TOMORROW: Jeff apologises publicly to Mary for not reading her fax.

St Coke's

Ecstasy Term begins today. There are 398 boys in prison. Miss Janet Street-Value (Uppers) is Out-of-Head Girl. L.S.D. Trip (Downers) is Keeper of the Pot. Mr Escobar Medellin has been made Head of Chemistry, replacing Mrs Marijuana Frostrup who is on a sabbatical in the Golden Triangle. Raves will be held in the school gymnasium every Friday, beginning at midnight. The orchestra will perform Mussorgsky's Night On A Magic Mushroom in the Frank Zappa Concert Hall on 24 November. The Timothy Leary Lecture will be given by the Marquess of Blandford on 27 November. The school play, *An Inspector Calls*, will take place after a tip-off and will lead to the arrest of the entire Sixth Form. Remands will be on 9 December.

Mr Gerry Adams An Apology

In recent years, in common with all other newspapers, we may have promulgated the erroneous impression that Mr Gerald "Gerry" Adams was in some sense the most evil man who had ever lived, responsible as he was for the deaths of a large number of innocent men, women and children.

Headlines such as YOU BASTARD, YOU MURDERING BASTARD and YOU BASTARD BASTARD may have led readers to draw the inference that we regarded Mr Adams, in the words of one of our own leaders, as "The Devil Incarnate".

We now realise that, on the contrary, Mr Adams was throughout this period a moderate statesmanlike figure working only for peace inside the democratic framework. We further accept that Mr Nelson MandAdams should be given the Nobel Peace Prize for his unstinting efforts to bring about a cessation of violence in the face of extremist pressure from some colleagues within the Republican movement.

We would like to take this opportunity to apologise to Mr Adams and to offer him a 12-page supplement entitled "St Gerry The Peacemaker".

TOP TEN BESTSELLERS

FICTION

1. Twelve Red Faces . . . . **Jeffrey Archer**
2. Not A Penny More Than £80,000 . . . . **Jeffrey Archer**
3. The Prodigious Sum . . . . **Jeffrey Archer**
4. Dishonour Among Thieves . . . . **Jeffrey Archer**
5. Beyond Any Doubt At All . . . . **Jeffrey Archer**
6. A Wallet Full Of Money . . . . **Jeffrey Archer**
7. A Twit In The Tale . . . . **Jeffrey Archer**
8. Kurd And Fable . . . . **Jeffrey Archer**
9. First Among Dealers . . . . **Jeffrey Archer**
10. As The Crook Lies . . . *(That's enough Bestsellers. Ed.)*

RADIO 5 LIVE

Announcer: And we now go over live to O'Malley's Bar and Bagel Parlour in downtown Chicago for an on-the-spot report on the historic IRA ceasefire…

Reporter: … and the atmosphere here is extraordinary. I'm witnessing scenes of jubilation not seen since… well, last night, when the Dodgers beat the Red Sox 187-136… it was one helluva night, I can tell you. Sir, you're an Irish-American, Mr O'Finkelburg — how do you react to the news?

Mr O'Finkelburg: Well, to be sure, Irish eyes are smiling tonight… It's a grand victory for the heroic freedom fighters of Old Blarney herself to finally drive the Redcoats out of Dublin led by Jackie Charlton and Sean Day-Lewis marching down Potato Avenue with a shamrock on their trilbies, a McGuinness in their hands, and a leprechaun on their shoulders with the proud green and purple flag of the Republic of …er… Haiti?

(Sound of man falling to floor)

Reporter: You, sir, Mr O'Mozzarella… Will you be going to Ulster for the celebrations?

Mr O'Mozzarella: Where's Ulster?

Reporter: It's in Ireland.

O'Mozzarella: To be sure it is, to be sure.

Reporter: And will you be going there?

O'Mozzarella: Don't be stupid. It's far too dangerous. People get killed there. Have you tried one of these pizzas? Just like Mama used to make back in old Derry…

(Sound of another man falling to floor)

Announcer: And now for further reaction we go live to O'Reilly's Taco and Tapas Bar in downtown Irish-Mexican Los Angeles…

(Continued 94KHz)

7

LABOUR SHOCK

I think you've taken the change of image too far, Tony

The Mail

ON SUNDAY — 65p

BLAIR 'WAS MEMBER OF LABOUR PARTY' — SHOCK REVELATION

by Our Smear Staff **C.N. Dee**

TONY BLAIR, the so-called darling of the chattering classes, was once a member of the extremist political group known as the Labour Party, we can reveal.

Records of the sixth form Debating Society at the Scottish public school McCakes Academy, reveal that the young Tony Blair once moved a motion "This house has no confidence in the Conservative Government".

Though not conclusive proof of his membership, this clearly links Blair with the hard-line, Ban the Bomb, TUC-loving Stalinist Bully-boys, lesbian mothers, flying pickets, you get the picture (continued page 94).

ON OTHER PAGES

Has the Blair Balloon Burst?
(No, Ed. But worth a try.)

NOBEL PEACE PRIZE FOR ADAMS?

by Our Irish-American Correspondent **Lunchtime O'Sitting Bull**

IRISH-Americans everywhere, from Ignorance, Arkansas, to Little Knowledge, Nebraska, are demanding that Sinn Fein president St Gerry of Adams be given the Nobel Peace Prize in recognition of his years of armed struggle in pursuit of his legitimate peaceful aims.

"He's the great peacemaker since Nelson Kissinger," said the influential Senator Slim Grasp O'History, spokesman for the Democratic Committee For Sucking Up To Gerry Adams In The Hope Of Winning A Few Votes.

Adams is believed to have been nominated for the top Swedish award by Sinn Fein themselves, but he faces stiff competition from Bosnian Serb peacefighter Radovan Murdovic, the leader of the Rwandan Hutu Peace Militias, Mr Machete, and last-minute entry General Slaughter, commander of the Haitian Death-for-Peace squads.

But Gerry Adams is confident of winning. Said a Sinn Fein spokesman: "If he does not gain his legitimate objective of winning the Peace Prize then he cannot be responsible for any subsequent bombing of the ceremony or murder of the judges by extremist factions."

"Beats me why we never thought of stacking them before"

"Not Thousand Island Dressing again!"

Prisoner found in jail shock

Reports from Whitemoor Prison suggest that in the early hours of this morning a prisoner was found in his cell by a vigilant prison officer.

"We don't know how this happened," said an embarrassed Governor. "The prisoner concerned was neither eating lobster nor building a bomb. We have no idea how this happened."

That Whitemoor IRA Gaol Menu in full

Paddy de Foie Gras
CavIRA On Toast
OR
Wild Gerry Soup

— ✳ —

Kneecap of Lamb
Chicken Kalashnikov
Sinn Fein of Beef with Paisley Sauce
Duck Not à l'Orange, served with All Greens
Permanent Peas and No Potatoes (due to Famine)

— ✳ —

Bombe Surprise
Semtexolina Pudding
Balaclava
OR
Choice of Rifles (shurely 'trifles'? Ed)

— ✳ —

Irish Coffee (Black or Tan)

— ✳ —

Cheeses
H-Block Cheddar
OR
Provolone

— ✳ —

From The Cellar
McGuinness (by the Pint)
Armalite Ale

— ✳ —

Warder Service Available

Last Night of the Prods

■ Many think this grand old British institution has had its day — the chanting, foot-stamping crowds waving Union Jacks, the well-worn old patriotic songs, the drums and penny whistles, the men in fancy costumes with their bowler hats and orange sashes being more British than the British.

But the last night of the Prods goes on and on, as much a part of the British way of life as a tandoori and lager.

Programme in Full

Land of Pope and Tory
Soloist **Dame I. Paisley**

Home Rule Britannia
Soloist **I. Paisley**

Londonderry Air (arr. behind closed doors by P. Mayhew)
Duet **J. Major** & **A. Reynolds**

God Save the Queen
(Broadcast on 94UVF)

SPONSORED BY HM GOVERNMENT

10.45pm BBC2
The Moral Bores

TONIGHT the panel addresses the conundrum "Why on earth would anyone put these people on television?" with Edward Beard from the *Guardian*, Janet Daley-Telegraph, David Stark-Raver and another man with glasses (possibly a don). Hosted by Michael Berk of 999 fame.

NEXT WEEK: "Should this programme be taken off?"

Schweitzer – was he the most evil man who ever lived?

Beginning a new series in which we offer a balanced reassessment of what total bastards everyone famous who lived in the past really were.

(Film clip of old man in pith helmet attempting to cure leper)

Voice Over: All his life Dr Albert Schweitzer lived in the African jungle attempting to alleviate the sufferings of sick Africans. At least that was his story. But today historians take a very different view.

(Cut to black American professor. Caption reads: DR LEROY PIPESUCKER, PROFESSOR OF AFRO-POLITICAL CORRECTNESS AT THE UNIVERSITY OF NEW DWORKIN*)*

Professor: Schweitzer exploited native black Africans without pity or mercy. His only interest was in acting out White Supremacist fantasies of the great European healer patronising poor Africans who were too sick to stand up to his Fascist colonialist oppression.

(Clip of old man in pith helmet floating down Congo with upright piano in canoe)

Voice Over: Many critics believe Schweitzer was one of the greatest organists of his time. But Prof. Pipesucker takes a different viewpoint.

Professor: Despite spending 50 years in the jungle, Schweitzer never grasped the polyrhythmic complexities of African drum music, but remained fixated on the decadent, musical sterile banalities of reactionary Euro-Christian German composers, such as the forerunner to Hitler, Johann Sebastian Bach.

(Clip of old man in pith helmet dying under mosquito net, watched by weeping Africans)

END

NEXT WEEK: *Reputations* looks at Taki Lotofcokeupthenos and discovers one of the most misunderstood geniuses of all time.

OWN BRAND H BOMBS

HUNTER

HURD AND MAJOR

(Silly music. Major is sitting at piano playing "When Irish Eyes Are Smiling". Hurd shimmies in with invitation on silver tray)

Hurd: I think you'll find, sir, you would have much more success with your piano playing were you to open the lid.

Major: What ho, Hurd. Ah, a stiffie! *(He grabs invitation from tray)* Who could it be from?

Hurd: I think if sir were to open it he would be provided with the necessary information as to the identity of the sender.

Major: Bally right again, Hurd! Must be all that fish you eat in the FO canteen!

Hurd: Possibly, sir.

Major *(tearing open envelope and reading)*: It's from some cove called Lord Archer! I wonder if he's related to my friend Oofy Archer who writes those dashed good books?

Hurd: I think you will find he is one and the same, sir. You will remember that you yourself elevated him to the peerage.

Major: Listen to this, Hurd… *(Reads aloud)* "Jeff 'n' Mary invite you, ie me, to Shepherds Pie and Fizz at the Tory Conference. Blue Tie compulsory!" Should be a jolly good binge, what?

Hurd: I dare say, sir, but I would venture to suggest that however jolly the festivities may turn out it would be inadvisable for you to attend. *(Begins to iron Major's straitjacket)*

Major: You old killjoy! Why?

Hurd: Well, sir, I am afraid your erstwhile friend has somewhat blotted his copy book; let the side down; put up a black mark.

Major: You don't say, Hurd! Oofy in some fishy business involving making a load of money in the City by reading his wife's fax? That doesn't sound like him *(pause)* or rather it does. *(Tears up card)*

Hurd: A commendable decision in the circumstances, sir, and I have taken the liberty of accepting an invitation from Mr Hanley instead on the night in question.

Major: What? Old Brain-Dead Hanley from the Drones? Jolly good! Carry on, Hurd.

(Major starts singing "Cock-ups and Mussels, Alive Alive Oh", whilst accompanying himself on the banjo. Silly Music. Credits)

The Alternative Rocky Horror Service Book

No. 94. A Service To celebrate The Opening On Sunday Of A Shopping Centre Owned By The Church Commissioners.

President *(suitably robed in t-shirt bearing legend 'JESUS SUPER-SAVER'):* Fellow consumers, we are gathered here today to give thanks for all the wonderful bargains available to customers of the Godco Shopping Mall. May I mention in particular *(here he or she may say "the Kiwi Fruit at only 69p" or it may be "6 Mini-Doughnuts at 99p" or it may be "the Wash'n'Go Shampoo Pack — 6 for the price of 4")*.

President: Let us give thanks to the Lord Sainsbury.

Congregation: For it is Meat and Veg over there.

HYMN

There shall then be sung an appropriate hymn, such as *"Queue up, queue up for Jesus"* or *"New every morning is the bread"*.

READING
(from the Gospel According to St Marks & Spencer)

"And there came unto him certain merchants, saying: 'Master, is it lawful to goeth unto the supermarket on the Sabbath day?' For they were hoping to catch him out. And he saith unto them: 'Yea, verily, for the Sabbath was not made for sitting around at home saying "What's the old film on the telly this afternoon? I wish we had cable." ' And he bade them go unto the markets and to fill their baskets with loaves and fishfingers, even an hundredfold. And they did even as he biddeth, and went on their way rejoicing."

President: Come unto me all ye who are heavy laden, and all the others go to the quick till for "6 Items Or Less".

All: I was in front of you.

(Then shall all the congregation proceed unto the tills, where they shall offer up a tithe of their week's wages as decreed by the Profit Asda)

THE RESPONSES

President: O Lord, open thou our purses.

Congregation: Do you take Switch?

President: We doeth indeed.

All: I can't open these sodding bags.

THE DISMISSAL

President: I am the Safeway (or it may be the Gateway), the truth and the life. Tesco in peace.

All: Thanks be to greed.

(Miss Samantha Fox will then make a personal appearance to sing her latest recording "Jesus Wants Me For A Sun Bird")

NEW IN THE EYE *(reprinted from the Daily Telegraph)*

VICTORIA CARGS

(daughter of famous columnist Alan Cargs)

ON MY way to school this morning I saw this newspaper placard, right? And it said "Peace At Last". So what?, I thought. Who wants peace? When it comes to Cricklewood, we've got more peace than we can handle.

I was playing my old techno-grunge-garage album at 2 o'clock the other morning (nostalgia or what?) and this old bat came in. And she's my mother, right. She said: "You're disturbing the peace." And I said: "Excuse *me*. You're disturbing my peace, so peace off." Talk about hassle. Forget Bosnia. OK? So I rang up my boyfriend and he agreed that people like my mum were a real pain. They've no idea what our generation thinks about anything.

☐ DO YOU know you can get really great bags in this new shop in Old Compton Street, opposite Clone Zone?

It's called Bags 'R' Us, which is a great name when you think about it.

I bet my Dad could write a whole piece about it in his column in *The Times*.

© *St Paul's Girls' School Magazine*

"I quite enjoyed it. Didn't you, asshole?"

YELTSIN HISTORIC VISIT TO IRELAND

Why don't you wake me up, you idiots?

Thank you for getting drunk with Aer Lingus. We hope you will get paralytic with us again soon

I hope there isn't a hiccup

Roll out the Boris

He's keeping a low profile

Poetry Corner

In Memoriam: Sir David Napley, Defender of Jeremy Thorpe

So. Farewell then
David Napley,
Solicitor to the
Famous.

You had a brown
Rolls-Royce and
Wore a
Bowler hat.

"My bill will be
A million pounds
Plus Vat."

That was your
Catchphrase.

Keith
Says:
"Rest in
Fees."

E.J. Thribb (aged 17½)

"I hope he does well — I have him in my Fantasy Chivalry team"

That Yeltsin Aeroplane Lunch menu in full

To start:
Vodka

— ✳ —

Followed by:
Vodka in Vodka
AND
Vodka
OR
Vodka

— ✳ —

From The Trolley:
Vodka with Vodka
OR
Vodka without Vodka

— ✳ —

To Drink:
Half-Pint of Old Mr Reynolds's Lemonade Shannon

Pompous. Pretentious. Puerile.

Is this Britain's most irritating man?

Wouldn't you like to biff Geoffrey Wheatcroft?

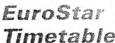

EuroStar Timetable

Get To The Continent Quicker Than You Dreamed Possible!

Waterloo-Paris

09.15	Depart Waterloo.
09.20	Enjoy three hours "dwell-time" at the new Waterloo "Euro-Shopping Experience" while waiting for train to be mended. Visit Le Tie-Rack, Le Sock-Shop et Le Burger-King.
12.15	Embus for Heathrow *(no surcharge).*
13.00	Bus held up by hole in ground outside Terminal 3.
14.00	Re-Embus for Gatwick.
15.30	Arrive Gatwick.
16.12	Take train back to Waterloo.
17.35	Arrive Waterloo and go home, having given up stupid idea of going to France.

eurostar

It's Quicker To Swim

IT WAS 3.32 in the afternoon. In an agreeable converted stable near Bath a phone rang. It was the Daily Mail features desk ringing up Geoffrey Wheatcroft, who was busy sleeping off his lunch.

"Geoffrey," said the voice from London. "We've tried everyone else — Paul Johnson, er... you know... anyway, but they've all said no so we're coming to you as a last resort. We'll make it worth your while."

"Of course I'll do it. What is it?" replied Wheatcroft.

"800 words on why you'd like to knock Stephen Fry's teeth down his throat for being a Leftie and a raving poof."

There was a brief silence. "Stephen Fry — is he any relation of my neighbour Jeremy Fry, Princess Margaret's friend?"

"No, Geoff, he's a comedian. He was nearly in a fight at some old boys' do. Anyway, don't worry if you've never heard of him. We'll fax you the cuts. We need it by four — that gives you 25 minutes. Thanks, Geoff — you're a white man."

THE celebrated man of letters took another draught of inspiration from the half-empty bottle of claret at his elbow. With great concentration he pulled a clean sheet of paper into his ancient typewriter and typed out, with one finger, the opening words of his article.

"Geoffrey Wheatcroft is a smug, unfunny, complacent bore and someone jolly well ought to beat him up," he wrote, before subsiding into his normal recumbent position.

But it was OK. The subs wrote the rest and once again the Daily Mail's Page Eight was a national disgrace *(surely 'talking point'? P.D.).*

■ Is there anyone on the Daily Mail that you'd like to hit hard in the face? Prizes of a blow-up-and-biff dummy of Sir David English or a case of Lagerlout Top-Strength Yob Brew to the best 10 letters explaining why you'd like to wallop editor Paul Dacre, Nigel Dumpster or any other top Mail name.

IS PEACE 'PERMANENT'?

by Our Historic Peace Accord Staff **Petronella Why-O'Wyatt**

IT was revealed last night that the Prime Minister had recently concluded a "secret deal" with his number one long-time enemy, Mrs Margaret Thatcher, during a behind-the-scenes lunch in St John's Wood.

This could herald an end to years of civil war that has raged inside the Conservative Party for so long.

Mr Major, however, is known to have reservations about whether the peace will be long-lasting, and is said to be seeking an assurance that Mrs Thatcher has laid down her handbag "on a permanent basis".

The deal, brokered by top intermediary Father Woodrow Wyfront (continued page 94)

"Terry, meet Mum and Dad"

HOW SHOULD TRAITOR HEWITT DIE?

Sun Phone Probe

A. String him up
0898 74324

B. Firing Squad at dawn
0898 748762

C. Injected with

Indian-style Plague
0898 92372

D. Forced to watch Mariella Frostrup video review programme on TV
0898 004246

RING NOW!!

THOSE MAJORS IN FULL

Major Ron
Disloyal, sleazy ex-officer trying to cash in on royal connections.

Major Hewitt
Disloyal, sleazy ex-officer trying to cash in on royal connections.

Major Terry Ball
Loyal, clueless former garden gnome manufacturer cashing in on connections to Prime Minister.

Major John
Sleazy, disloyal ex-Chancellor trying to cash in on royal connections (Margaret Thatcher).

Major Tom
Silly spaceman trying to cash in on connections with Ground Control.

Major Mates (formerly Colonel)
Sleazy, disloyal ex-Colonel trying to cash in on connections with Asil Nadir.

Major Roadworks
Sleazy, disloyal *(We get the picture – Ed)*

New Books this Autumn

1. It's All Her Fault by Prince Charles *(as told to J. Dimbleby)*. Snipcock & Tweed, £29.99.

2. It's All His Fault by Princess Diana *(as told to A. Morton)*. Bloomsbury, £39.99.

3. No It Isn't, You Bitch by Prince Charles *(as told to anyone who will listen)*. Oxford University Press, £49.99.

4. Fook Off, You Fooking Bastard by Princess Diana *(as told to James Kelman)*. Fuckworths, £79.99.

(That's enough books. Ed.)

That Upper Class
BLIND DATE
— In Full —

(Enter Cilla, walking down steps in turquoise-and-marmalade mini-skirt and high heels)

Cilla: O-o-o-o-h! Have we gorra lorra lovely geezers and one extra-special lovely, lonely lass tonight! *(Audience cheer wildly)* Let's meet our first contestant, all the way from Kensington, Diana. Let's girra a big hand! I'd bet you'd like to, fellas!

Audience: Oooh! Saucy!

(Music. Enter Princess of Wales in slinky low-cut ballgown)

Cilla: Don't you look just like a princess, chuck?

Diana: Ya, I do actually, 'cos I am. OK?

(Audience go hysterical, waving Union Jacks)

Cilla: Now, behind that screen we've got three smashin' lads who'd all like to spend an evening with you — candlelit supper for two, and… who knows?

(Audience shout "MI5!". Shot of three smirking upper-class twits on stools, clutching mobile telephones)

Cilla: Which of this trio of likely lads will get lucky tonight? Will it be Number One…

Voice over: Oliver Hoare, millionaire art-dealer and expert in Islamic ceramics.

Cilla: Oooh, posh! Or will it be gorgeous Number Two…

Voice over: James Gilbey, car salesman and member of the celebrated gin family.

Cilla: Oooh, 'e sounds like a real tonic!

(Many members of audience die laughing)

Cilla: … or hunky Number Three?

Voice over: Guards officer Major James Hewitt, who plays polo…

Cilla: Oooh! Hello Chucka!

(Complete silence from studio audience, who do not understand joke)

Diana *(reading from card)*: My question to Number One is: "Why didn't you answer the phone, you bastard?"

Oliver Hoare: because my wife was there.

Cilla: Oooh, cheeky!

(Audience cheer)

Diana: This is for Number Two. If you called me up from the car late at night, what pet name would I use?

James Gilbey: Oh, I say, do I have to answer this? I would like you to call me something soft and floppy — like 'Squidgy'!

Audience: Oooh!! Squidgy!

Cilla *(nudging Di)*: Oooh! He found that a hard one to answer, didn't he?

(The remainder of the audience are carried out in hysterics by paramedics)

Diana: And, lastly, Number Three. If I went to bed with you, what would you do afterwards? Would you a) smoke a cigarette? b) roll over and go to sleep or c) cuddle me until dawn?

Major Hewitt *(laughing)*: I would sell the story to the highest bidder. Ha ha ha!!

(Audience cheer and shout "We want to read it!")

Cilla: That's it, our Di! The choice is yours. Which is it going to be? Munchy Number One, Scrunchy Number Two, or Dirty Number Three?

Diana: I want them all.

(Randy men burst out from behind screen, removing trousers)

Cilla: Aaaah! Aren't they a luvverly foursome? And now let's see how last week's couple got on. Arianna Stassinopoulos and Senator Huffington-Puffington went to Washington on their Blind Date in the hope of becoming President and First Lady of the United States.

(Silly music)

ENDS

"Let us through! We're ordinary members of the public with floral tributes"

Lives of the Saints
№ 94

THE TEMPTATIONS OF ST CHARLES MOORE

ONE of England's most loved holy men, St Charles lived at the top of a tower in a remote corner of London.

One day a vision appeared before him in the shape of a beautiful young woman, calling herself Anna Pasternak.

"I am a ghost," she said. "I can offer you something that will bring you fame and fortune and boost the circulation of the *Sunday Telegraph* to at least three copies."

"No," said the saint. "Not another picture of the proprietor's wife in a mini-skirt?"

The apparition shook her head beguilingly. "Far, far sexier than that," she replied.

The saint meditated long and hard. "You don't mean", he stammered, "you can deliver me Mariella Frostrup's *Sunday Times* column, complete with a photo of the columnist in a revealing, low-cut dress?"

Again the waif-like temptress shook her dainty head. "Charles, baby," she said. "I am offering you the biggest scoop in the entire history of the world. But before I can disclose what it is, you must sign this confidentiality agreement."

The saint wrestled with his conscience for all of fifteen seconds, and signed.

"Now, Chazzo," said the tantalising phantom. "Here's the deal. I can give you the bloke who bonked Princess Di, in his own words, all the dirty bits, exclusive to the *Sunday Telegraph* for only £250,000."

All the torments of the nether region crowded round the holy man as he fought manfully with the temptation that had been presented to him.

On the one hand, he had always been prepared to go on *Newsnight* and attack Andrew Neill for this sort of thing.

But on the other, if he gave way, he would be blessed in the sight of his Master, King Conrad the Black, for putting up the sales.

What was he to do? For minutes on end, the saint writhed and squirmed on the satanic horns of this fearful dilemma.

But then he jumped from his chair and shouted: "Be gone, demon! I will have none of your unholy pact. Instead I shall appear on *Newsnight*, and write in the *Spectator*, telling the world of how noble I was to renounce your filthy offer."

NEXT WEEK: How St Jeffrey of Grantchester helped a poor Kurd to make £80,000 after hearing voices on the telephone.

Peter McLie

The World's Worst Columnist

I HAVE discovered a most delicious new food which, like so many good things to eat, comes from the shops.

It is not much to look at, to be sure — brown, round and knobbly, like my friend Andrew Wilson's knees after he has been playing hockey for his club.

But just slip one of these versatile vegetables into a pan filled with boiling water, and three hours later you have a dish fit for a king!

You can mash them, fry them, bake them or even toast them. And each way is as good as the last.

I confidently predict that soon every household in the country will be feasting on this delectable new treat.

It's name is the pineapple. Remember you read it here first!

I CANNOT help noticing how many people are sporting a poppy in their buttonholes these days. What a strange choice of flower to choose! Is it a sign of Freemasonry? Or are all the wearers members of the so-called Gay Community? Surely not, because even my friend Andrew Wilson is wearing one.

I have a better idea. Why don't we all wear poppies on a certain day in memory of those who fought and died in the Great War? And we could call that day "Fireworks Day". *(You're fired. Ed.)*

VERY OFTEN the final paragraph of a column is very short and has no ideas in it.
Why is this, I wonder?
Perhaps I shall never know.
(Brilliant stuff, Peter. Keep it up. — S.S.)

"Oh, do play us a medley of your hit, Mr Gorecki"

UP FRONTERS

Continuing the hugely popular Sunday Colour Supplement
you can read exclusively in every paper…

Some Enchanted **Eve**? That's what **Max** is singing along to **Lady Pollard**! Looks like she's going to Bust his Record! But shouldn't she let **Bygraves** be **Bygraves**? Anyway, they make a lovely couple!?

Surely she's beyond our **Ken**! We thought **Miss Frostrup** wasn't the **Mariella**-ing kind. But perhaps they'll just be **Livingstone** in sin! What a Little Picture Show that would be — and wouldn't **Ken**'s face be Red!

Double O dear! Who does **Sean** think he's **Con-nery**-ing? Stick to James Bond because your outfit is looking pretty old hat! You should spend a Moneypenny or two on a decent pair of trousers! Oh Dr No!?

Don't **Conti** your chickens before they hatch, **Tom**! You might get a cold front from Weathergirl **Miss Johnson**!! On the other hand it might well be **Ulrika** on the Night! Shirley she'll end up as your Valentine?

I've been **Di**-ing to meet you! That's the message from Harrods boss **Mohammed** to the **Princess of Sales**!! I'd take your hand off her knee or, as they say in newspapers, you're **Fayed**!? *(You're fired. Ed.)*

Clapton your hands! Here comes **Eric**! He's Unplugged at the moment but that could change if **Miss Frostrup** proved the **Mariella**-ing kind. *(You've done that one. Ed.)* Anyway, she looks like a cat that's got the Cream! Perhaps he fancies a pluck! That'll make a great Little Picture Show! *(You really are fired this time. Ed.)*

Snow-u-Like!
1 Rouble for
1000 tons!

Arctic News

FRIDAY NOVEMBER 4 1994

Pick Up A Penguin!
Only 200 Roubles
each

HUGE SLEAZE SPILL THREATENS TO WIPE OUT BRITAIN

by Our London Staff **Eskimo Nell Hamilton**

AN ENORMOUS slick of crude greed is washing out of Westminster after a leakage in the Guardian newspaper led to vast quantities of unadulterated filth being spilt.

Rescue workers, led by Mr John Major, are desperately trying to stem the tide of sleaze, but the clean-up campaign has come too late to save the lives of at least two endangered species.

The almost unknown Smith has gone, and the Spotted-In-The-Ritz Hamilton has, after a short struggle, been wiped out.

Fears are growing for hundreds of others who are in it "up to their necks", according to one Observer (sold to Mrs J. Fenby).

"The Aitken could be next," claimed an environmental specialist. "They are spraying on these fancy deterrents, but it won't wash." He continued: "Once the river of muck gets going, there is wave after wave of grime, and it all sticks."

It looks as though this is worse than the sinking of the Torrey Archer or even the Sexxon Mellor disaster. This could be the biggest natural catastrophe in Britain since John Major became Prime Minister.

EXCLUSIVE TO THE EYE!

That fake Guardian fax that fooled the Ritz

Horse of Commons

Office of Mr Jonathan Aitken P.M.

Dear The Ritz,

Could you please send me, as soon as prissible, a coipu of my boll for the night of 17 September *(check sub)* when I strayed with yuo.

I want this bill so that the Gruniad can expiose me as a lair, a chate and a merchant of slooze.

Send immediately to Mr Peter Pratson, Oditor, The Grandiad, Farringdon Toad, Londin.

PS. This is not a fake fax. Honstely.

A STATEMENT FROM MOHAMED AL-GNOME

If the Government accuses me of blackmail, I'll really spill the beans

Remember: Top People Are Shopped At Harrods

MP ADMITS 'I FAILED TO GET SNOUT IN TROUGH'

**by Our Political Staff
Dominic Harrods**

THE WORLD of Westminster was rocked to its foundations yesterday by the discovery that a Tory backbencher, Mr Tim Goodfellow, MP for Lymeswold South, had never committed any form of impropriety since he was elected in 1992.

Our enquiries reveal that Mr Goodfellow has never once:

● been paid £1000 to ask a parliamentary question

● stayed in the Ritz Hotel at the expense of a Middle-eastern entrepreneur

● fathered a love child by a woman other than his mistress

● rented his basement to a Miss Whiplash

● accepted hospitality from persons connected with any terrorist organisation

● engaged in 3-in-a-bed love romps with the wife and daughters of anyone at all

● accepted a £12 million consultancy fee from a Middle Eastern potentate

● enjoyed the services of a clairvoyant masseuse

Leading members of Mr Goodfellow's party were last night reported to be "shocked and dismayed" by the depths of the depravity to which he had not sunk.

His wife Christine Goodfellow has decided not to stand by him. "I have suffered enough," she said.

From The Desk of Mr Peter Carter-Fuck

Dear Sir:

The above article regarding our putative client Mr Tim Goodfellow MP has been drawn to our attention by myself.

I am hoping to represent Mr Goodfellow when I have rung him and told him that he has an overwhelming case for demanding a full apology and very substantial damages for the allegations recklessly disseminated by your article. The suggestion that my client was in some way so professionally incompetent as to fail to take advantage of the opportunities for self-enrichment open to him by virtue of his position as a member of parliament is beyond a peradventure the vilest and most unconscionable libel I have ever had the pleasure of reading.

*Yours faithfully
P. CARTER-FUCK
(aged 125)*

That Neil Hamilton Paris Ritz Menu in full

Hors d'Office

— ✳ —

Dans La Soupe

— ✳ —

*Stuffed Wallet à l'Egyptienne
Barefaced Cheek of Lamb
Honeyroast Hamilton
All Served with Pommes Freebee and
Fresh Green Sleaze*

— ✳ —

*Hard Cheese
Sour Grapes*

— ✳ —

Not In The Cabinet Pudding

— ✳ —

To Drink:
Saint Tenmillion Dans La Poche

OR

Questions-In-The-House Wine (£3,000 extra)

— ✳ —

(Bill to M. Fayed, copy to P. Preston, The Grauniad)

SLEAZE AND WHINE PARTY

IT COULD BE YOU.

All you have to do is get the right numbers of votes in the election and — hey presto! — you're well on the way to becoming a millionaire.

Just look at these fabulous prizes that could be won if you're a Tory MP:

● **£500,000 directorship of recently privatised amenity!**

● **£300,000 in consultancy fees.**

● **Luxury weekends in Five Star Parisian splendour!**

● **Toe-jobs by unemployed actresses** *(shurely 'wealthy viscountesses'? Ed)*.

● **Holidays in Majorca with charming PLO hostesses.**

● **And much, much more!**

Said one lucky winner, a Mr Smith (who wanted no publicity but got plenty and then got sacked): "All I had to do was ask a simple question about Harrods and — bingo! — I had wads of cash stuffed into my pocket!"

Getting rich has never been so sleazy! *(Shurely 'easy'? Ed.)*

THE NATIONAL LO-TORY™

MPs IN NEW MEMBERS' REGISTER SHOCK

by Our Sleaze Staff
Ian Greed

OVER nine hundred members of both the House of Commons and the Lords last night changed their entries in the Parliamentary Register of Members' Interests.

When interviewed, all of those concerned claimed that the timing of their move was "entirely coincidental" and had nothing to do with the Prime Minister's concerns about the so-called "Sleaze Factor".

A typical change was that of Dame Angela Rumbusiness, whose entry formerly read:

INTEREST: Making a huge amount of money by working for shady lobbyists.

It now reads:

INTEREST: Saving my skin before it is too late.

"It is a matter of setting the record straight," said Dame Angela Rumpole, "in case people come to the wrong conclusion about what I am doing. My interests are essentially the same — i.e. myself — but I thought it was important to clear the air at this point.

"In fact I am so concerned about this issue that I am willing to ask questions about it in the House — if you make it worth my while."

Dame Angela Rumbled is 72.

"How can we be sure that you're Roy Orbison
and Buddy Holly?"

The Doggie Telegraph
O.J. Dempsey Trial Continues

By Our Crime Staff J.S. Bark and Sir Alfred Bite

THE TRIAL of the accused pit bull terrier O.J. Dempsey at Bow Wow Street magistrates court today entered its 1,027th day.

Proceedings came to a halt when Mr Justice Cockerspaniel ordered defence lawyers to produce the now-famous blood-stained muzzle which, it has been alleged, Dempsey was wearing when he was arrested.

Reign of terrier

Earlier, defence counsel for Dempsey, Mr Hartley Redsetter, claimed that his client had been a victim of anti-pit-bull-terrier prejudice. "There is no doubt in my mind," he told the jury, "that if Dempsey had been a pure-bred English sheep dog he would not be facing Death Row today."

Videos were produced in which Inspector Nipper of the Yard was heard uttering inflammatory snarls, to the effect that "all pit bulls should be taken

to the vet and put to sleep. It is the only language these mad dogs understand."

There is increasing concern in legal circles that the Dempsey trial, which is being followed by 2 billion dogs all over the world, is making British justice a laughing stock.

INSIDE ■ Play the new Doggie Lottery — and Winalot 6 ■ Paul Johnson writes "Bow, Oh Wow" 9 ■ Extremely Funny Cartoon by Mutt 11

Mr Travolta and friend
share a joke

Marquess Shooting Party

I RUN into an old friend, the Marquess of Cholmondeley, at the Garrick Club. The Marquess is in fine form, regaling me with tales from his days in the Guards. I listen with amusement and then blow him away.

Grave Concern

TO LADY Sabrina Gosforth's delightful estate in Gloucestershire, accompanied in the boot of my car by the late Marquess of Cholmondeley. I take the opportunity to bury him in a shallow grave where I am unexpectedly joined by the delightful Lady Sabrina and her guard dogs. She asks me what on earth I am up to. Alas, I have to blow her away too. And the dogs as well!

Pulp Fiction

A PARTY at Grosvenor House to celebrate the launch of Pippa Darlington's new biography of her aunt Lady Edith Tregunter, published by HarperCollins.

I meet Pippa, who asks why I am covered in blood and carrying a sawn-off shotgun. To her polite enquiry, I jovially riposte: "Don't fucking fuck with me, you fucking fuck."

I make my excuses and leave her bleeding to death on the carpet.

Home Sweet Home

I RECEIVE a call at home from the police, who surround the house and ask me if I would be interested in throwing down my weapons and joining them at the station to assist with their enquiries. Instead I turn on the flamethrower and torch them all alive. What japes!

Cutting

☐ From the Wivelsfield Examiner, a reader has kindly sent me this cutting: Man fries wife, cuts off ears and jumps in acid bath!!!

Quentin Letts is on holiday

Lady Cobhamley's Lover

(adapted for TV by Barbara Mills and Pat Boon)

(Scene of stately home in Midlands, Ragley Hall. Cut to library where aged peer in tweeds is reading Daily Telegraph to large dog)

Lord Cobhamley *(for it is he):* I say, Towser, I don't get the point of this joke by Garland. Can you explain it to me?

(Enter butler with double whisky on server)

Butler: Will that be all, sir?

Lord C: I say, Wheatcroft, have you seen Her Ladyship?

Butler: She's gone to one of her Heritage meetings, My Lord. She said not to wait up for her.

Lord C: That's a relief. I'm glad the little woman has found an outside interest at last.

Butler: You can say that again, My Lord. *(Winks at dog)*

(Lord C falls asleep over article by Simon Heffer on privatisation of the post office. Cut to wooded glade on Lord C's estate. Lady C, looking blonde and randy, wanders provocatively into glade to find toothy, virile, working-class ex-Cabinet Minister hacking away at his latest Guardian piece about funding for provincial opera houses)

Lady C: Ah, Mellors, how are you getting on with that piece?

Mellors *(laughing rudely):* Oh, I've finished with her and her toe-sookin'. Now, 'appen, I'm ready for a bit of upper-class tottie like thysen'.

Lady C: Ooo, you are awful.

(Takes off clothes)

Mellors *(gazing at her naked form):* Aye, 'appen, as an 'eritage expert I can tell thee tha's got a grade one well-preserved frontage on thee, and no mistakin'. Thee and I is going to be an item, I warrant thee.

Lady C: What sort of item?

(Several hacks from News of the World leap out of bushes)

First hack: An item on next Sunday's front page, that's what you'll be!

(Excited journalists rush off with scoop. Cut back to library at Ragley Hall. Lord C is reading Telegraph to heads of various dead deer on walls. Enter Lady C, looking dishevelled but happy)

Lord C: I say, darling, I see you're in the papers with that frightful little fellow Mellors. Never liked the cut of his jib, wandering around the estate with his trousers down. Talk at the club was that he was mixed up with some Arab bint. What does it mean?

Lady C *(bursting into tears):* It means that David and I have forged a bond.

Lord C: What? Forgery? Bonds? This sounds suspiciously like my friend Lord Archole.

(Mellors enters through french windows, pursued by pack of wild journalists)

Mellors: Nay, the bond of true love, Your Lordship. Thy wife and I have come to know each other, in the fullest, deepest, blood-sense of the word. We 'ave enjoyed the deepest, fullest mystical Communion that only a man and a woman can knowst. Obviously my first concern is my family and my constituents, who have incidentally given me their full support.

Lady C: As has my husband — haven't you, darling?

Lord C: Whatever you say, my dear. *(Resumes studying Telegraph 'Quick Crossword')* I say, before you go, you wouldn't happen to know a four-letter word beginning with 'F' meaning 'To have full, deep, blood-communion with someone else's wife', would you?

Mellors: Fook. Off.

© D.H. Lawrence, 1994.

CAST IN FULL

Lord C	LESLIE PHILLIPS
Lady C	MARIELLA FROSTRUP
Mellor	ROBBIE COLTRANE
Butler	STEPHEN FRY
First hack	SIR DAVID FROSTRUP

Directed by Ken Russell Twisk

The Alternative Rocky Horror Service Book

No. 94: Service of Holy Matrimony for the Third or More Time to be used by Clerks in Holy Orders.

President: Nice to see you all again.

All: To see you, nice.

President: Who giveth this vicar to be married for the *n*th time?

(Here he may say 3, 4, 5, or 94, as the case may be)

Ex-wife: I do. She's welcome to him.

(The congregation may then laugh)

Vicar: Can't we shorten this? I've got to conduct a wedding myself at 3.30 p.m.

President: Very well. Let's face it, this is the twentieth century after all.

Congregation: Indeed it is.

President: Is there any just cause or impediment why these two serial monogamists should not be joined in Holy Intercourse?

Bishop *(standing at back of church):* I object!

President: Objection overruled. You are out of touch with modern Christian beliefs. Our Lord Himself was married many times.

Bishop: No he wasn't.

President: Yes he was.

All *(sing):* Ooh-Aah-Cantona!

President: I now pronounce you Vicar and 3rd Wife.

All: Great! Terrific! *(or they may say "Nice one, Vicar" or "Come on down")*

President: You may now divorce the bride.

(The congregation shall then sung the Departing Hymn No. 94, 'I'm Getting Re-Married in the Morning' from the HymnalongaHolloway Song Book)

© Church of England 1994.

NEW MELLOR SHOCK

Hello, darlin' — fancy a quickie?

Lives Of The Saints

No. 94: Saint Christopher of Hitchens

FEW PEOPLE had heard of this obscure saint who for many years lived the life of a recluse in America. Only occasionally could he be seen emerging from his anchorite's cell on Lower 58th Street to appear as the "token left-winger" on chat shows in return for large sums of money.

But then came the miraculous event which was to make St Christopher famous for at least a day. He was sitting in a bar when he was approached by an Eastern holy man, the Blessed Tariq of Bandung. The guru said to him: "Arise, Christopher, you have holy work to do this day. You have been chosen by Channel Four to go out into the world and expose a false prophetess, who has millions under her thrall. If you do this, you will win the thanks of mankind and a more than earthly reward — viz. you will be the centre of a great controversy for at least ten minutes."

All Is Vanity Fair

And St Christopher beseeched him, saying: "How can I do this, when I am only an humble hack, unworthy of this great task you are calling me to? What's the money like?"

And Tariq said: "It is good. And we will give unto you a researcher, who will do all the hard work." And the Western saint said "It's a deal."

And so it was that, shortly afterwards, St Christopher was able to expose to the world the most evil woman who had ever lived — Mother Teresa of Calcutta.

St Christopher revealed to an astonished world that this infamous old woman was nothing less than a Roman Catholic nun who believed in God.

NEXT WEEK: Stalin Reassessed. Was the hated Russian dictator really St Alin of Georgia, who only killed millions of people for their own good?

TONY, TAKE FRANKIE AND ROCCO AND GO PICK UP GINA

IGOR PETROVICH, TAKE DIMITRI DIMITRIEVICH AND ANDREI FILIPPOVICH AND... OH FORGET IT, I'LL DO IT MYSELF

AMERICAN MAFIA   RUSSIAN MAFIA

GLENDA SLAGG

Fleet Street's Queen of Common Sense

PRINCE CHARLES!?! Aren't-cha-sickofhim!!? According to the Prince of Wails (geddit?) everyone else is to blame for his sorry plight?!?! OK, so his dad bullied him — so what? He obviously didn't hit him hard enough or he wouldn't be a-whingin' and a-cringin', a-moanin' and a-groanin', a-blubbin' and a-blabbin' *(Get on with it. Ed)* to TV's Jonathan Dimbleby!!?

Who wants a wimp on the throne?! Not this lil loyal subject — that's for sure!?! Go back to your polo, Prince Charmless, and leave the book-writing to your wife!!?!? OK?!?

WHY'S everyone suddenly got it in for Prince Charles?!? It can't have been much fun havin' Philip The Terrible as yer dad!?! No wonder Charlie looks like a puppy who's been left out in the rain! Come and have a little weep on Auntie Glenda's shoulder!?! We love you, Your Maj-to-be, and we all want *you* to wear the crown!? Vivat Charlie Boy! Hoorah for Big Ears!

THREE cheers for the Duke of Edinburgh!! Here's a man who's not frightened to give his son a good hiding just cos he's unhappy at public school!?! Thank goodness someone still believes in old-fashioned fatherhood. My dad used to take a belt to me when I was small and it's made me what I am today!?!? Phil The Fearless, we salute you!?!? Bully for you!!? (Geddit?)

DON'TCHA feel sorry for the Queen?!? As if poor old Lizzie hadn't got enough trouble with her wayward kids, she has to put up with a child-abusing monster as a hubbie!?! Beware of Greeks bearing whips is my message!!?! (Geddit?) No wonder HRM has run off to Russia to drown her sorrows with Mr Yeltsin. Dos Vidanya, Ma'am!?! (That's Russian for "Bottoms up", stoopid!)

GOR BLIMEY!?!? What the flippin' heck does the Queen think she's doing now!?! Flyin' off to Moscow when her son's about to top himself!?! Call yourself a mother?! You need your husband to beat some sense into you, jus' like my dad did to me dear ol' mum!?!? Never did 'er any harm, may she rest in pease.

PRINCE Charles!?! Arentcha-sickofhim?! *(You've done this. Ed.)*

HERE THEY are, Glenda's Gorgeous Gladiators!?!?

MARK THATCHER. How would you like to spend a night in *my* arms, Big Boy?!? And it won't cost you £12 million?!? Is it a deal?!?

JAMES KELMAN. Booker's Mr Foul-Mouth!?! Why not drop round and give lil Glenda a ****?!?

ED PEARCE. The Moral Maze's Nr Munchy?!?

Byeeeeeeee!!!

ADVERTISEMENT

ROYAL NATIONAL SHAKESPEARE COMPANY

A M.idsummer Night's Dream

by William Shakespeare

"A stunning new production"
SUNDAY TIMES

"Innovative, exciting and exhilarating"
THE GRAUNIAD

"Unmissable"
TIME OUT

RNSC

At the Young Barbican from September

"Make up your mind, Fishbeard — are you a pirate or a surrealist?"

WHAT NAME DO YOU THINK THE ROYAL FAMILY SHOULD TAKE? *YOU DECIDE:*

Windsor	0898 347271
Windsor-Mountbatten	0898 347272
Saxe-Coburg-Gotha	0898 347273
Squidgy-Windsor-Davies	0898 347274
Coburg-Tampax-Parker-Bowles	0898 347275
Holstein-Pils-Spencer	0898 347276
Peregrine-Worsthorne-Carbuncle	0898 347277
Montgomery-Massingberd-Evostick	0898 347278
Windsor-Tie-Rack	0898 347279
Mariella-Frostrup	0898 347270

Calls are charged off-peak at £38 per minute

Exclusive Extract from the book by Jonathan Dimbleby, 'The Prince Gets His Own Back'

That Mountbatten Letter to Charles in full

Dear Charles,

You asked me for my advice as to what you should do re the fair sex.

Well, let your wise old uncle pass on the benefit of his experience.

Sow your wild oats for as long as you can before you tie the knot.

Then find some innocent young gel to marry who is too sweet to know what you are up to.

Then carry on with the oats.

Believe me, you can't go wrong. Trust your old Uncle Dickie, and the House of Windsor will remain as safe and sound as the ship I skippered during the war. *

Your devoted "granpa",
DICKIE MOUNTBATTEN OF BUMADVICE

*The HMS Kelly was later the subject of Noel Coward's famous film *In Which We Sink.*

Song of the Sea

Ro-ro-ro the boat
Quickly under water.
Ferrily, ferrily, ferrily, ferrily,
The firm gets off manslaughter.

(Traditional)

NEW WORDS

by Philip Howard

GROBBELAAR
n. (slang) under-counter payment, backhander, often given in brown envelope. Example: "I'll meet you in the hotel room and bung you a nice little grobbelaar." (*Martin Chuzzlewit*)

PRESTON
n. man who occupies senior job for many years for no apparent reason. Example: "That Trelford was a bit of a preston." (*UK Preston Gazette*, 1991)

RUMBOLD
v. intrans. to be caught out taking grobbelaars in the political arena. Example: "Damn, I've been rumbold. But I won't resign until I have to." (*Hansard*)

BLAIR
v. hot-air device for filling balloons. Example: "Turn up the blair, old man, or we'll end up crashing into that field full of pigs." (*The Archers*, 1994)

"Come on, Mona darling, give me happy... That's it... Maybe laugh a little... Perfect, make love with the canvas... Yes, keep it going..."

Lines On The Dismissal Of Mr Andrew Neill By Mr Rupert Murdoch

by William Rees-McGonagall

'Twas in the year nineteen hundred and forty nine
That there was born the greatest journalist of all time.
It was from the bonnie town of Paisley that the great man
came
And, as all the world now knows, Andrew Ferguson Neill
was his name.

But Caledonia's fair lochs and glens could not contain
Young Andrew's genius, so he got on a train.
He bade farewell to the land of Highland mist
And came to London where he got a job on The Economist.

But it was not long before this brilliant young figure
Caught the eye of the man all Fleet Street knew as
The Dirty Digger.
And in one of the fastest ever of journalistic climbs
He was promoted to the prestigious job of Editor of
The Sunday Times.

Soon all the nation was talking about this whizz-kid of
a lad
Whom the so-called wits of Private Eye enviously dubbed
"Brillo Pad".
This was a reference to his mop of frizzy wire-wool hair
Which looked like one of those scouring devices that
people keep in packs under the stair.

Along with light bulbs, buckets and bottles of carpet
stain remover
And also of course those little paper bags you put in
the Hoover.
All the world agreed that he was a dashing and
handsome fella,
And soon he had attracted a dusky beauty called Pamella.

Night after night they would dance at a disco called Tramp
Where you would not find people like Sir Peregrine
Worsthorne or Gavin Stamp.
Indeed these carryings-on soon became the subject of a
very famous case of libel
When Sir Peregrine went into the box and swore on the
Holy Bible.

"No self-respecting editors of Sunday papers
Should be seen in a night club performing vulgar capers.
They should be like myself, sitting in the Garrick Club,
Talking about the Maastricht Treaty over traditional
English grub.

"A typical menu of the day might be
Brown Windsor Soup, Roast Beef and a glass of Chateau
Lafite 1973.

But, instead of mixing with Archbishops and Lords,
Mr Neill chooses to cavort with the shameless
Miss Bordes."

Anyway, that was all a long time ago.
But it is the only thing about his editorship that we
all know.
Except of course that he exposed the marital problems of
Prince Charles and Diana
And went on TV to defend himself against Charles Moore
in a very courageous manner.

Nothing else that he did occurs to me
Except that he had a talk show on the station LBC.
This fired young Andrew with the desire to be a media star
Or a famous chat show host like America's legendary
Jack Paar.

So he packed his bags and caught the Concorde for
New York,
Hoping of that town too he would soon be the talk.
Mr Murdoch promised him fortune and fame
And that on American TV he would make his name.

The great media tycoon outlined his master plan.
"Brillo," he said. "You will be my network's anchorman."
But, alas for our hero, when he made his pilot,
It was under "G" for Garbage that the Americans chose
to file it.

New Yorkers could not understand a single word that
the Scotsman said.
And they were also baffled by what seemed to be the
dead sheep on his head.
After his first show, he went to bed feeling pleased but
tired.
Until the phone rang at 2 a.m. and Mr Murdoch said:
"You're fired."

"Please, sir," said Andrew, "can I have my old Sunday
Times job back?"
"No," said the Digger. "From that too you have got
the sack."
And so he pulled the plug on poor old Brillo,
And left him sobbing into a lonely pillow.

The only job left for Andrew to do
Is to present a show in the middle of the night on BBC2.
And, as befits his new status as a lowly hack,
To write articles for the Daily Mail somewhere near the
back.

© William Rees-McGonagall 1994.

LOTTERY DRAMA

Gas worker wins 6-figure payout

by Our Utility Staff
Bamber Gascoiningitin

"IT WILL CHANGE MY LIFE!" chortled Yorkshire-born Gas Board official Cedric Brown, 59, who yesterday claimed a record £475,000 payout from himself in the latest Government lottery.

Speaking from his humble 15-bedroom mansion in Buckinghamshire, a clearly delighted Cedric explained to reporters how he arrived at his winning number.

What A Lottery I Got

"I was sitting around talking with a few mates at work when the idea suddenly hit me — why don't I get a huge sum of money?

"The next thing I knew, they'd all

agreed and told me to name my figure.

"I chose £475,000 because it just so happened to be the amount of money I wanted to have."

Mr Brown asked for "no publicity", but unfortunately all the papers found out.

ADVERTISEMENT

ESSO-S!

There's a keeper in your tiger!

For Better Zookeeping Try Aspinall's!

NEW LUCAN THEORY SHOCKS NATION

by Our Lucanology Staff
Sir Ludicrous Kennedy

IN A television documentary to be shown tonight, leading criminologists will present a radical new explanation for the mystery of the murder of Lord Lucan's nanny exactly 20 years ago.

The claim that will amaze viewers is that the killer was none other than Lord Lucan.

"I know it sounds ridiculous," says the programme's producer. "but in the course of our investigations it became increasingly obvious that he did it."

There were apparently five key points that led the investigators to their stunning conclusion.

- He did it.
- He ran away after he did it.
- He never came back after he did it.
- No one else did it.
- He did it.

There is, however, one remaining mystery which the new programme fails to explain:

- Why are there hundreds of programmes on the television about an unpleasant upper-class murderer who clearly did it twenty years ago?

"I was thinking the very same thing the other day — what did happen to Bananarama?"

ST CAKE'S HEAD LASHES LEAGUE TABLES

by Our Educational Correspondent
John Mortarboard

MR J.R.T. KIPLING, headmaster of St Cake's, the prestigious £10,412-a-term Midlands public school, yesterday hit out at the "disgraceful distortions" thrown up by the government's league tables for schools.

St Cake's appeared in 2,816th place in the Department of Education's chart showing the exam record of Britain's 2,816 schools.

Cross Head

"The whole basis on which these tables are computed", said Mr Kipling, "is extremely unfair and gives a totally misleading impression.

"For instance," he went on, "no allowance is made for the quality of intake. It is all very well to point out that no St Cake's students passed their GCSEs last year, but I am forced to recruit all our pupils from the upper classes, many of whom come from broken stately homes and are generally very intellectually challenged, i.e. thick.

"Some of our boys can scarcely read the titles on the videos which they spend all their time watching."

Exceedingly Bad Cake's

Mr Kipling, himself an Old Cakeian, said that his school was at a gross disadvantage compared to schools in the inner cities, with their open recruitment policy.

"How can my pupils compete with all these bright Asian kids, who do their homework and pass exams? It is ludicrous to compare my school with a comprehensive."

BRITAIN'S BOTTOM TEN

2810			31	+14
2811	Hanger Lane Gyratory College, Hounslow	22	−13.2*	−12.0
2812	Ken Livingstone School, Neasden	21	+3.0	−4.0
2813	Nelson Mandela High, Toxteth	20	+2.6	17.0
2814	Marcus Garvey Technical College, Balham	16	−4.2	12.0
2815	Robert Maxwell Academy, Oxford	8	−6.3	30.0
2816	St Cake's	0	−112.3	0

All these figures are meaningless

"Geese are very good for keeping the grass down"

HONEYSETT

THE HOLLYWOOD REPORTER
$2.50

English Magazine in Sinister Conspiracy Shock

by Our Hollywood Staff **Lunchtime O'Jews**

THE Hollywood Reporter can exclusively reveal that the English magazine The Spectator is run by a secret cabal of "Twits".

The "Twit conspiracy" is well-known in English media circles but until now no one has dared to speak out. But it is time the truth was told. Just look at the surnames of the people involved in the Spectator — Lawson, Cash, Johnson, Moore, House Chancellor, Nicholson, Palmer, Taki, Applebaum *(Shurely shome mishtake? Ed)*.

The surnames say it all. They're Twits. And they are typical of their kind. Upper-middle class, snobbish, lazy, mean and given to making absurd generalisations about everyone else.

William Cashin

Using their positions of power at the Spectator, these Twits extend their clandestine network to give patronage to other Twits and to exclude anyone who can write or who has anything interesting to say.

Said one Non-Twit who was too scared to give his name: "I have been trying to get into the Spectator for years, but instead Dominic Lawson keeps printing fantastically bad pieces by William Cash. Why? Simple. Because they are fellow Twits of course."

Old Goy Network

The excluded journalist continued: "Don't get me wrong. I'm not anti-Twitic. Some of my best friends are Twits. I just think that someone should point out the truth, ie that these people have a stranglehold on British life. If you're a Twit, it's a passport to the Telegraph, the Sunday Telegraph, the lot! They're everywhere! We've got to stop them before it's too late!"

Coming soon in the

THE SPECTATOR

More William Cash Exclusives

Do the Jews run Israel?

Is the Pope a Catholic?

Do bears shit in the woods?

(Shurely another mishtake, Ed.)

© The SpectacularlySilly

THOSE GOTT-KGB SECRETS IN FULL

by Our Spectator Staff
C.I.A. Lawson

WE CAN now exclusively reveal the amazing secrets that Soviet superspy Richard Gott passed on to his KGB paymasters from his key position at the heart of the Guardian.

● At the height of the Cuban missile crisis in 1963 Gott sent the following report to the Kremlin:

"There is a new group called The Rolling Stones who are undermining capitalist society by advocating unrestricted hedonism. It is only a matter of time before the glorious day comes."

Gott was rewarded for this highly-prized information by a free lunch at Jimmy's Greek restaurant in Soho.

● At the height of the Vietnam War in 1972, Gott again supplied Stalin with vital intelligence:

"The Tories are back in power. It is a sad day for the proletariat. We must all work harder to overthrow capitalism and its evil works, ie flared trousers and kipper ties which are also in."

Gott was fêted for this by his Russian handlers and given a free subscription to Izvestia.

● At the height of the Falklands War in 1982, from his new post as Guardian Literary Editor, Gott was able to supply full details of the secret Booker shortlist weeks before it was widely available. It included the names of Beverly Whittington, P.F. Drom, Mosinka O'Dinka, Craig Fitte-Pryce, Sharon Jill and Melvyn Bragg.

The last name was a mistake and a furious KGB stripped Gott down to the rank of full Colonel and withdrew his name from the Free Luncheon Voucher List at the Soviet Embassy.

● In the Nineties Gott re-established his pole position as the KGB's top mole during the Gulf War of 1991. At the height of Desert Storm Gott tipped off the Russians that:

"The Guardian has promoted Peter Figgis to Assistant Night Editor (Sports) over the head of the hated Sean Beard thus opening up the possibility of recruiting Figgis, a known SDP supporter, to our cause. Comrade Brezhnev should be delighted that the Guardian is giving a lead once again in the inevitable destruction of the doomed military-industrial complex."

For this Gott was hit over the head by an unknown assailant in a fur hat who said "Take that! You idiot." Peter Preston meanwhile promoted Gott to *(That's enough secrets, Ed)*.

"Flintstein? Too foreign. Flintstone's more American"

UNIVERSITY CHALLENGE

(Silly music and titles)

Paxman *(for it is he):* This week the teams are Balliol College Oxford and the University of Neasden, formerly the World of Carpets in Brent. And the starter for you, Balliol, is: recite in full the 13th century Papal Bull denouncing the Albigensian Heresy.

(Buzzer sounds. Man with glasses and unconvincing beard begins to recite in Latin)

Man with beard: Pontifex ego maximus, Innocentus Deo…

Paxman *(sneering):* Oh come on! That's the vocative tense there. Completely wrong. I can't allow that. I'm not going to offer it to Neasden because there's no point. So, Neasden, here's your first question — and, to make it easier, it's multiple choice.

(Shot of four mature students, reading VIZ [shurely 'sociology'? Ed])

Paxman: Is the Prime Minister: a) John Major? b) Bono from U2? c) Vivienne Westwood?

(Buzzer goes)

Voice over: Grunge, Neasden.

Grunge *(for it is he):* Is it Paul McCartney?

Paxman: Well, close enough. It begins with an 'M'. 100 points to Neasden.

(Continues in similar vein for 30 minutes)

It's so simple

What happens, Mr Cholmondley-Warner, is that Mercury hire a very expensive celebrity for their advertisements

I see, yes

And then find that they've paid him so much that there is none left for their workers

Mmm. That makes sense

So they have to sack them all

And then they sack the celebrity

Fuck!

Goodbye Mr Grayson

GCSE English Literature

3 Hours (or as long as you like)

Paper One

Read the following extract from the Canterbury Tales by Geoffrey Chaucer and say what you think about it.

The Camilla's Tale

A ladye was there hyght Camilla Parker-Bowles
Who of the maydenhead of Engelond was the fairest of all soules.
Married was she to a soldier brave and true
A Colonel of the Guardes was he, yclept Andrew.
Upon the comely dame a Prince did cast his eye
And saith to her, "With thee, fair wench, I wish to lie."
And so the twain were soon enclasp'd in bed
Though each of these wightes was to another wed.
Her snow-white breastes made princely passions rise
Till e'en the butler heard his lecherous cries.
"My Prince," quoth she, "to thee I plight my troth;
So long as our love stays secret twixt us both."
Imagine then her great dismay to see
Her lustful lover appearing on TV,
Sitting in his garden without his jacket
Boasting how he had placed a hand upon her placket.
"By St Loy," quoth she, "to be a King this tattlemouth's not fytte,
Forsooth, for telling all, he is an A1 shytte."

SOMETHING TOLD THE POSTMAN THIS WAS
GOING TO BE A DIFFICULT CHRISTMAS

30

HURD AND MAJOR

(Silly music. Hurd is hanging Christmas decorations, while Bertie Major strums piano and sings… "My old man says follow the VAT…" He breaks off, looking puzzled)

Major: I say, Hurd, these Serb johnnies seem to be getting a bit restive, trampling over jolly old Bihac and generally cocking a snook at brother UNPROFOR.

Hurd: Sir seems to be unusually well informed this morning. I hope sir isn't feeling unwell.

Major: Heard it on the wireless. Jolly useful gadget.

Hurd: Indeed sir. I am sure Mr Birt would be most gratified by your sentiment, dedicated as he is to his "mission to inform".

Major: Well kindly inform *me*, Hurd, as to why we seem to be making such a bally hash of things. I thought we were meant to be waving the big stick and keeping friend Serb cowering in his bunker while our chaps buzz around overhead zapping them with the odd bomberooni, eh what?

Hurd: Indeed a colourful scenario, sir. But sadly, as so often is the case, the realities of the situation are more complicated.

Major: Come again, Hurd?

Hurd: If we take punitive action against the supporters of Mr Karadicz, sir, they might well feel disposed to retaliate against our own soldiers.

Major: Well, can't out chaps just jolly well shoot back, Hurd?

Hurd: Oh no, sir. Our men are not allowed to fight. They are only there to keep the peace.

Major: Then why did we send soldiers in the first place — why not just a load of lollipop ladies to dish out the soup?

Hurd: I don't think, sir, that flippancy is appropriate, given the very unhappy plight of the poor Bosnians.

Major *(chastened)*: Well, if you're so clever, Hurd, with all that fish you eat, what's your plan for getting us out of this mess?

Hurd: The time has come, sir, when we must draw a firm line. We must issue an ultimatum to Mr Milosevic and his friends.

Major: You mean, Hurd, we're going to get really tough at last?

Hurd: I fear so, sir. There is no alternative, as you will recall your Aunt Magatha was fond of remarking.

Major: Jolly good. So, what do we tell them?

Hurd: I suggest, sir, that we issue the strongest possible warning to the Serbs that, unless they agree to our peace plans, we will take all our soldiers home and leave them to sort it out for themselves.

Major: Gosh, Hurd, that is a really top-hole solution to the whole bally problem.

Hurd: I always endeavour to give service, sir.

(Major returns to piano and sings: "If you were the only Boutros Boutros-Ghali in the world…")

CSA SWOOP ON ABSENT FATHER

Lapland 25 December

INSPECTORS from the Child Support Agency conducted a lightning swoop this morning on a snow-covered grotto near the North Pole where they served a maintenance order on a Mr Christmas.

Santa Maintenance Clause

They alleged that this man with the long white beard is in fact the father of millions of children round the world.

Said one inspector, Ms Dawn Raid: "This man is a disgrace. He calls himself a father but he only visits them once a year and tries to buy their affection with presents. He never answers their letters and refuses direct contact with them by creeping down the chimney in the middle of the night."

Last night Mr Christmas refused to comment, saying: "Ho ho ho ho ho ho ho!"

LETTERS TO THE EDITOR

From Sir Herbert Gusset

SIR,—In the light of the recent spell of unnaturally mild weather may I share with your readers what I saw in my garden on December 15th?

To my amazement, I first noticed tulips flowering in the herbaceous border beneath a majestic palm tree which had not been there the night before.

Imagine my surprise when I saw my wife picking avocadoes from the tree which formerly bore crab apples. Walking further into the shrubbery I discovered swallows nesting in the orchids and several pink flamingoes disporting themselves by the ornamental pond which, I have to say, was full of alligators.

I rang my friend, Buffy Frobisher, to see if these freak climatic conditions had replicated themselves in his garden, but I was told by his lady wife that Buffy had sadly been eaten by cannibals earlier that morning.

At this precise moment I heard the first cuckoo of Christmas and decided to take refuge from the ensuing desert sandstorm in the Lamb and Flag, where I remain.

Yours sincerely,
SIR HERBERT GUSSET,
Delirium St. Tremens,
Booker-on-Mail,
Somerset.

GETTING RELIGION BACK INTO CHRISTMAS

UPFRONTERS

We're Manwatching you, **Mr Morris**! It's pretty **Clare** that **Desmond**'s got his eyes on Agony Auntie **Rayner**!! You must be off your tree! Anthropologise to the lady at once, luvvie!!!

"Ooh-ah-you?" asks Weathergirl **Suzanne Charlton**. **Cantona** you see that it's **Eric**? Careful with your tackle, Monsieur, or she'll tell her dad — and he's a **Bobby**!! He'll stop you getting United!

Don't give up the **Chase**, mate! You're **Caine** and **Lorraine**'s Able!! Not a lot of people know what you're up to! Could be that she's only taking the **Michael**!! *(You've done this 100 times. Ed.)*

Sophia so good! These Hollywood Heroines are **Taylor**-made to be friends! That's show-**Liz**! And **Loren** may they last! *(You're fired. Ed.)*

Baddiel luck, **Emma**!! You're dancing the night away with the other hunky humorist **Rob Newman**!! Did you find him in the **Thompson** Directory?!? But surely, **Mrs Branagh**, he's years your junior!! Bet he'll feel like a **Newman** in the morning!? It's beyond our **Ken**! *(I told you you're fired. Ed.)*

What a **Charlie**! Why didn't they tell the Prince it wasn't fancy dress? Perhaps because no one fancies him! In that outfit you should be **Di**-ing of embarrassment! How po-lo can you get?! *(This is so bad you can have your job back. Ed.)*

HURD AND MAJOR

(Silly music. Bertie Major is at the piano strumming "Let's All Be Beastly To The Gormans". Hurd in background irons the Christmas wrapping paper for re-use next year)

Major: I say, Hurd, after all that turkey, what the taste buds are after is a spot of good old English fish, eh what?

Hurd: That may indeed be the case, sir, but I fear it is no longer possible.

Major: You mean you brainy coves have swallowed the lot?

Hurd: Not exactly, sir, although it was the noted classical physician Galen who first drew attention to the relation between cerebral activity and the consumption of the piscine species.

Major: Dashed clever, those Greeks. I bet they eat a lot of fish.

Hurd: Indeed, sir. Though I fear that nowadays it is the gentlemen from the Iberian peninsula who have established something of a monopoly in that respect.

Major: What? You mean that's why there's no more fish left for our chaps to catch? Chips are going to look pretty silly on their own. How on earth did this come about?

Hurd: You may recall, sir, that you sent off your friend Mr Waldegrave to save Britain's fish from all being bagged by our European neighbours?.

Major: What? "Oofy" Waldegrave? He wouldn't know a fish if it came up to him in the street and said "Good Evening".

Hurd: On the contrary, sir. Mr Waldegrave had the inestimable benefit of being educated at Eton.

Major: Well, he should have 'eton' more fish. Do you get it, Hurd?

Hurd: Indeed I do, sir. And very amusing it is, too, sir, if I may say so.

Major: So, we sent Oofy off to do battle with johnny dago. And what happened then?

Hurd: Well, you will recall, sir, that on the last occasion when we took on the Spaniards, at the time of the so-called Armada, we won. This time Mr Waldegrave decided that it would be diplomatic for us to come second.

Major: I say! Good old Oofy! Bloody clever. Must have eaten a lot of fish down at the Drones before he went off. They do a dashed good Dover Sole there, Hurd.

Hurd: Not any more, sir.

(Major plays "Rule España, España Rules The Waves" while Hurd opens tin of Rabbit-and-Liver Whiskas for supper)

© Fry and Laurie, from an idea by P.G. Wodehouse

"I can't make my mind up — another pint or go home and surf the Internet"

COURT CIRCULAR

KLOSTERS

His Royal Highness the Prince of Wales will take a cup of espresso coffee at the Schneeblick Bar and Carvery at 2500 metres. He will be escorted by HRH Prince William, HRH Prince Harry and Nanny "Tiggy" Legge-Over. He will studiously ignore Her Royal Highness the Duchess of York when she tries to get a table adjacent to his. But HRHs William and Harry will grant an audience over a Sno-Cola to HRHs the Princesses Eugenie and Beatrice. In attendance will be Mr James Whitaker, Mr Sleazo Papparazzo and other distinguished members of the international press corps. The Prince of Wales will then get in a bate and ski off, attended by the cameras of the BBC and ITN. Later he will meet Nanny Legge-Over and give her an "innocent kiss" in full view of the world's press. He will then get in another bate.

VAIL, COLORADO

Her Royal Highness the Princess of Wales will be inviting herself to stay with a number of unknown American millionaires. They will include Morton J. Assetstripper and Harvey Wallbanger III. She will be hoping to meet the press at any opportunity in her desire to embarrass HRH the Prince of Wales.

BUCKINGHAM PALACE

A statement will be issued denying that Miss Legge-Over is in any sense a replacement for Princess Diana. "Charles kisses her in public and obviously likes her. It couldn't be more different."

WINDSOR

Her Majesty the Queen will not be amused by any of the above. She will then watch a video recording of her Christmas Broadcast and congratulate herself on the wisdom of not having mentioned her eldest son, or indeed any of her other children, during the programme.

KENSINGTON PALACE

The Duke and Duchess of Gloucester, accompanied by Messrs Eric, Sam and Dave from Pickfords Removals, will arrive and install themselves in their new home. There will be a short argument about missing pictures and broken crockery during which Messrs Eric, Sam and Dave will shrug their shoulders. The Duke will then resolve the dispute by indicating that the taxpayer will pick up the bill anyway.

CRUISE TURNS SOUR FOR HONEYMOON COUPLE

'Pea-green boat should never have put to sea' claims Owl

by Our Maritime Staff
Connor No Cruise O'Brien

A FURIOUS couple had their "dream trip" ruined when the luxury vessel that they had booked for their holiday of a lifetime turned out to be a "floating nightmare".

Said Mr Owl: "My fiancée, Ms Pussycat, had saved up to go on a 366 day cruise, including a stop at the Land where the Bong Trees Grow, but the brochure gave no indication of the seaborne hell that we were to suffer."

Unhappy New Lear

The owl's complaints included:

● **Inadequate catering:** "Only one jar of honey was provided for the whole trip and the owners tried to fob us off by wrapping it up in a five-pound note."

● **No entertainment:** "There was no international cabaret at all. Instead, I had to improvise songs on my own guitar to keep my partner happy during the long night hours."

● **Lack of care:** "Even when we arrived at Bong Tree Island there was no proper reception with grass-skirted maidens singing, as we had been led to believe. Only a pig turned up to meet us and tried to sell us a cheap brass ring from Ratners."

● **Crew shortages:** "We were meant to be married by the Captain in the 1st Class Lounge. Instead, we had to make do with a turkey officiating. The only food on offer at the reception was mince and slices of quince which we had to eat with a totally unsatisfactory utensil called a runcible spoon."

The owners of the vessel, however, denied the couple's claims. Said a spokesman: "The owl and the pussycat are just whingeing. We operate a number of other vessels full of satisfied customers, including the S.S. Sieve, which is currently on a special 'Jumbly' cruise to Changly Boor. Any allegations that the Sieve is leaking and generally unseaworthy have been wildly exaggerated by the Media."

The Q.E. is 2.

"Maureen, could you pass me one Domingo, one Carreras and a Pavarotti..."

HOWARD ESCAPES
No One To Blame

by our Prison Staff
Lunchtime O'Screws

ONE OF the world's most dangerous men, Mr Michael Howard, last night escaped for the 89th time.

Howard is still on the run after serving only two years as Home Secretary.

A top secret report has revealed that Howard's treatment was "extremely lax" and that it was "no surprise to anyone" when he wriggled yet again out of the hole he was in.

Howard's Away

The report claimed that Howard was:

● **given large sums of money to spend on lunches with journalists to whom he told "his story"**;

● given 24 hour a day use of a chauffeur-driven limousine from the government pool;

● on Christian name terms with many of Britain's top policemen;

● allowed to mix freely with top politicians, including the Prime Minister.

The report also pointed the finger at Howard's chief keeper, Mr John Major, who failed to supervise Howard's dangerous activities.

Not Howard's End

Major had often been warned that Howard was a very serious "security risk", and that he might do something "very silly" at any time.

But Major turned a blind eye — with the catastrophic results that all Britain is having to live with.

I'm going to lock you up and throw you the key

PORRIDGE

A hilarious new comedy starring Derek Lewis, Director of Prisons.

There is no security problem. My job is very secure!

HK! HA!

I'm here for life. And I believe that means life!

HO! HO!

But if you've got any complaints, my door is always open!

HA! HA!

STOP THIS INHUMAN TRADE NOW

Waldegrave row continues

by Our Agricultural Correspondent
Andrew Veall of the Sunday Times and Daily Mail

ANIMAL rights protestors again picketed the House of Commons to protest against the appalling treatment of Mr William Waldegrave, described as "a dumb animal kept alive in terrible conditions".

The protestors claim to have seen a pallid Waldegrave put in a train from Somerset where he was crammed into a restaurant compartment with four other men in suits reading the *Telegraph*. "They were fed only on the InterCity Sizzler which, as everyone knows, contains no nutrients at all."

Veal Eat Again

They claimed that Waldegrave was then unceremoniously packed into a pen or bench in the House of Commons where he was forced to sit day and night with other pathetic creatures all shouting and braying with panic.

But Waldegrave's owner, Mr Major, refuted the claims of cruelty. "Waldegrave enjoys it," he told reporters. "He has been bred for this very purpose — at Eton. If we let him out he would be a danger to himself."

Protestors were unconvinced. Said one: "Mr Waldegrave has been reduced to a whimpering wreck who does not even know the time of day. He is kept in the dark and fed nothing but rubbish."

Mr Major had the last word. "It is silly people getting sentimental about Waldegrave. He is for the chop shortly and it doesn't matter how I treat him since he is going to be destroyed anyway."

Mr Waldegrave is £2,000 per pound.

NEWSNIGHT

with Jeremy Paxman

(Pompous music)

Paxman: The Director General of the BBC Mr John Birt has made a dismal speech today suggesting that BBC interviewers are aggressive and rude. I have the little jerk here in the studio.

Birt: Good evening.

Paxman: You're meant to be the Director General, aren't you?

Birt: Er…

Paxman: Oh come on! Either you are or you aren't…

Birt: Well, yes, now you put it like that, I suppose I am.

Paxman: Haven't you got the guts to tell me face to face that you don't like me rather than making some speech in Dublin?

Birt: No. No sir. It's more of a general point I was making.

(Birt adjusts Armani tie nervously)

Paxman: You're pathetic. Get off.

Birt: Thank you very much, Mr Paxman.

Paxman: Next week the University of Toxteth will be taking on Francine Stock.

(Silly music)

"Congratulations, it's a quango"

MAN WITH GLASSES LEAVES JOB

by Our Financial Staff
Screaming Lord Saatchi

IN A MOVE which left the City gasping, a man in a suit and glasses yesterday left his job.

World financial markets were left reeling by the incredible news that the man in glasses had decided to resign.

In a shock fax delivered to anyone with a machine, Mr Maurice Suitchi, who with his non-bespectacled brother gave his name to the most legendary ad agency of all time, Suitchi and Suitchi, told the firm's now weeping employees why he had decided to leave.

That shock fax in full:

> Dear Guys with Ponytails and Blondes with Flipcharts.
>
> It is with a heavy heart that I am being fired. The new management have been out to get me and now they have. I will treasure for ever the privilege of working with each and every one of you. I feel uniquely blessed to have sat at my desk for 25 years and made wonderful amounts of money, thanks to your talent, creativity, genius and loyalty. I love you all. God bless you.
>
> Mr. M. I. Suitchi

So ended the greatest era advertising has ever known.

The Suitchi Legend — Their Finest Adverts

VOTE CONSERVATIVE	DON'T VOTE LABOUR	VOTE CONSERVATIVE AGAIN
1979	1981	1983
LABOUR ARE USELESS	ER…	THAT'S IT
1987	1992	1994

"I've just had a great someone else's idea"

Answers to Quiz Of Year

1) Mariella Frostrup.

2) Stephen Fry, Michael Portillo and Ian McKellen. All the others have moustaches.

3) a) If Jeffrey had invested £250,000, he would have made £80,000 for himself
   b) 3 years' imprisonment.

4) Ernest Saunders, Ronald Reagan, Harold Wilson. One of them does not have Alzheimer's.

5) i) David Mellor
   ii) Mellors
   iii) Mel Smith.

6) Odd one out:
   i) Ronnie and Reggie
   ii) Kevin and Ian
   iii) Bonnie and Clyde.

7) Bruce Grobbelaar, Terry Venables, George Graham, Neil Hamilton.

8) i) 12½ inches
   ii) Major Hewitt
   iii) Princess Diana.

9) Picture Quiz
   a) Dominic Lawson
   b) Mark Lawson
   c) Dave Lee Travis.

10) Mariella Frostrup.

(That's enough Quiz. Ed.)

A Cabbie writes

Every week a well-known taxi driver discusses an issue of topical importance. This week: **Kevin Stothard** (Cab No. 375501).

See about that bloke West who murdered all them women and then paved 'em all in? 'E's only gorn and topped himself, hasn't he? Bastard! He's cheated justice, hasn't he? Now there won't be a proper trial or nuffink. I was really lookin' forward to readin' all about that. Bloody cheek! Now we'll never know what 'e done. I mean, 'e probably murdered 'undreds of people and now he's just got away with it. I tell you what we should do wiv blokes who try that on — string 'em up. It's the only language they understand. I 'ad that Dennis Nilssen in the back of the cab once. Very nice bloke, as it happens.

NEXT WEEK: Melvyn Marckus (Cab no. 951) on why Ernest Saunders should be let out (surely 'strung up'? Ed).

"It's his last bit of DIY"

THE TIMES

FRIDAY JANUARY 27 1995

"Yo! Gimme one!"

Civil War in Saatchnia worsens

BY OUR REALLY IMPORTANT STORY STAFF KATE ADS

REBEL forces in the strife-torn capital of Saatchnia were today digging in against a counter-attack by forces loyal to the former Saatchni regime. Fierce battles have been raging in the boardroom, corridors and wine bars around the besieged headquarters of the self-styled President of the Saachnis and writs have been raining down like mortars on rival combatants.

I have seen grown men weeping over their sacked comrades and women wandering about in a daze, trying to find loved ones who have been given large redundancy payments.

"The world cannot just stand by and watch Saatchnia fall apart," said one 21-year-old account executive I met, who was clearly suffering from post-lunch-stress disorder. "Surely Saatchnia deserves better than this?"

Meanwhile the long queues of refugees heading out of the Saatchni warzone tell their own story.

Said one elderly fat man with a cigar, who would only give his name as 'Lord King': "We cannot stay. It is not safe here for the British Airways account any more. It is a tragedy."

Only one question remains as Saatchnia descends into a living hell in front of the averted eyes of the international community. "What on earth is a story about admen doing on the front pages of national newspapers?"

A Doctor writes
Alzheimer's Disease

AS A Doctor I am often asked "Is Ernest Saunders innocent?" The simple answer is of course not.

What happens is that the public experiences a mild form of collective Alzheimer's Disease or *Guinnus fraudus forgetfulous* as it is known to us doctors.

As a result of this the country begins to suffer from delusions, including a belief that Saunders and his friends were only convicted on some technicality and that it was all a long time ago.

The only known treatment for this failure of memory is to go back and look at the facts — ie they were all in it up to their necks.

If you suddenly find yourself forgetting that Mr Saunders is guilty, you are probably a member of the European Commission and should seek medical advice at once.

©A. Doctor

TV Highlights — BBC2

Was Richard The Sweetheart in fact a Warrior King?

HISTORIAN Terry Jones examines controversial new evidence which seems to show that the celebrated homosexual, mass-murderer Richard I may also have been a closet King of England.

"You won't believe it," promises TV's whacky ex-Python turned Regius Professor of Modern History. "I'm lifting the lid on one of the most disgraceful episodes in English History — ie why I am given licence payers' money to romp around in fancy dress talking bollocks."

STAR RATING: One to Miss.

While recording *Abbey Road*, there were signs of growing animosity between John and Paul

LA DAME AUX CAMILLAS

**A new saga from the pen of SYLVIE KRIN, authoress of
Heir of Sorrows and Love in the Saddle.**

CAMILLA looked into the gilt-edged mirror, with its inscription "To Mrs Parker-Knoll, from the officers and men of the 17/31st Queen's Own Vets, Singapore 1/3/59".

How long ago it seemed that her husband's regiment had presented it to her on Ladies' Night. The heat of that tropical evening. The white-robed *bamigboys* bringing in the ice-cold rum frostrups on silver salvers…

And how things had changed.

She tentatively allowed her finger to explore the lines round her eyes.

"Laughter lines", Charles had called them. But recently, it seemed, he had given her precious little to laugh about.

Her marriage was over. She had become a public laughing-stock. And she could not even leave her beloved 18th century Wiltshire mansion, Placket Grange, without running the gauntlet of hundreds of evil-smelling journalists.

She even knew them by name now. There was "Reg", with the whisky breath, from the Sun. "Eddie", with the whisky breath, from the Mirror. "Quentin", with the whisky breath, from the Independent.

And then there was the worst of them all — the balding man from the Mail with the flared trousers, who was always pretending that he knew them. What did they call him? "Dumper"? "Dumpstrain"? Something like that.

How long would she have to endure this lonely nightmare? A prisoner in her own home. Would no one rescue her? Would her prince never come…?

THE PHONE trilled by the bedside. Automatically her hand went out. "Charles, hullo, is that you?" "No, it's Peter Costelotte here." At once she recognised the silken tones of the senior partner of London's oldest-established divorce lawyers, Costelotte & Lose of Paternoster Row.

"The other side has been most co-operative, Mrs Parker-Knoll. The decree nisi sailed through in jiffy. You, of course, can go on living in the house until it is sold. We were very fortunate that the, er, co-respondent, His… er… Royal… you know…"

The elderly lawyer coughed nervously, as if afraid to mention the true author of all his client's miseries.

In the pregnant silence, Camilla's gaze strayed to the photograph in its silver frame by the bedside. There he was, in his polo kit, laughing casually, with the hand-written message: "To Gladys from her ever-loving Neddy (Seagoon)."

"… what I mean, of course, is that we were very lucky that the third party in question made a full and frank admission of his adultery on national television."

From outside in the park, as dusk fell, came the drunken chanting of the hacks. "Come on, Horseface, get your tits out for the lads…"

Camilla shuddered with distaste and drew the curtains. To think that a few fleeting moments of happiness under that *Flowering Tampaxia* at Highgrove had brought her to such humiliation.

Truly she had paid the price.

"Of course," continued the suavely spoken lawyer, "the price of your house should help to take care of the little matter of our fees. As to your future maintenance, I think we can say that the way is now clear for you to contract another, er, marital arrangement, should you of course so desire. Ahem.

"We were attacked by Native Americans!"

May I, madam, wish you the very best of fortune in your new life? And may I humbly remind you that you have 30 days to pay our bill before interest is incurred."

The line went dead. Camilla slowly replaced the receiver.

"Yes," she thought. Perhaps the lawyer was right. Perhaps she would now be able to start again. In spite of the odd wrinkle here and there, she was not that old.

She still dressed well. At least her friends told her so. Elegant, was the word used by her hairdresser, Monsieur Kevin of "Uppercut" in Chippenham.

Surely the path was now clear for Charles to follow her example? After all, it was two years since he and his neurotic bride had formally separated.

Besides, attitudes had changed. It was quite acceptable now. Not like in the days of Edward the Fox and Mrs Simpson.

Everyone got divorced nowadays. Why, even the Archbishop of Canterbury did it. Or was it his children?

Her hopes soared like the sap rising in an old rose bush, as a long hard winter gives way to the first warming rays of spring sunshine. And could there be the distant promise of summer, and an Abbey wedding?

Flags being waved by the little children at the roadside. Street parties. A special stamp from the GPO. The smiling face of her regal mother-in-law graciously welcoming her at last into the bosom of her family.

"You were always the one we hoped he would marry."

Ding-dong, ding-dong, ding-dong. A thousand church bells sounded their message of rejoicing in Camilla's excited reverie…

…Tring, tring, tring tring. It was only the phone again.

"Hello, is that Mr Costelotte?" she answered expectantly.

"No, it's me, Charles," said that familiar voice, which at once set her heart pounding. "Look, darling, I can't be long, I've got one of my Trust meetings, but I've been thinking about… er… us…"

Her legs turned to jelly. "Us?" she breathed, hardly daring to imagine what he was about to say next.

"Yes, well, I think we'd better put a bit of a lid on the whole thing. These polls in the Sun and the Star. It seems the public just aren't ready for, you know, you and me as an item."

Camilla sank onto the bed. Her world was once again in tatters.

"Does that mean, Charles," she stuttered, "that I'll never see you again?"

"No, of course not. I expect I'll still be popping round now and again for a spot of you-know-what. Ha, ha ha."

His hollow laughter hung on the air.

FROM the lawn outside there was the sound of voices raised in excitement. "Here, lads, look at these family snaps I've just nicked from the piano in the drawing room. There's one of her, starkers. She's only three, but it's her alright." "Brilliant!" a chorus of voices answered. "Hold the front page."

Camilla gazed once again into the mirror. The face that stared back at her seemed to have aged a hundred years.

© Alexander Dumas

Poetry Corner

In Memoriam
Lord Kagan

So. Farewell then
Lord Kagan.

Gannex raincoat king and
Friend of
Lord Wislon.

"Not guilty."
That was your catchphrase.

But you
Were.

E.J. Thribb (17½)

To the Editor of the Daily Telegraph

The Lottery

From Sir Herbert Gussett

SIR—Many of your readers will no doubt have been outraged, as was I, by the sight of Sir Jeremy Isaacs and the well-heeled fat cats of the Covent Garden Opera House queuing up to collect billions of pounds of our money from the so-called National Lottery.

Meanwhile, down here in the provinces, the arts are literally starving to death through lack of funding. I am thinking of small groups of performing artists such as our own Lamb & Flag Players, who specialise in a once-yearly gala performance of highlights from the best-loved operettas of Messrs Gilbert and Sullivan, with assistance from the "karaoke" device operated by our landlord, Mr Montague Balon. Surely it is enterprises such as this which constitute the true lifeblood of the arts in England today? What price the £1 million-a-night Signor Pavarotti singing Rigoletto's famous 'La Donna e Mobile' when you can hear such items as these:

'A Wandering Minstrel I', sung by Lt-Col Buffy Frobisher, accompanied by the Rev. Purvis (pianoforte).

'Three Little Maids From School Are We'. Male voice trio (Gussett, Frobisher, Balon; counter-tenors).

'Für Elise' (first half). Pianoforte solo played by Lady Letitia Gussett.

'Four And Twenty Virgins (Came Down From Inverness)'. Trad. Sung by H. Gussett, unaccompanied.

It is for the chance to perpetuate this great cultural tradition that we have made a formal application to the Minister for Lotteries for the paltry sum of £700,000. But what chance have true amateurs like ourselves got against the metropolitan clique of Mr Isaacs and his mink-coated merchant bankers? Long live G and T *(surely 'S'? Ed)*.

Yours faithfully
H. GUSSETT
'Unprofor'
Carter St Ruck
Dorset

"Ladies and gentlemen, we are sorry to have to announce that Mrs Eileen Prosser of Market Drayton, who was to sit in seat F4 of the amphitheatre, is indisposed this evening. Her place will be taken by Miss Joyce Willis of Bletchley. Thank you."

BLAIR'S NEW POLICY SHOCK

by Our Blair Staff
Smiles Kington

THE LEADER of the Labour Party, Mr Tony Blair, made a controversial speech last night outlining his new policy on having policies.

"Some people in this party have accused me of having no policies at all.

"This could not be further from the truth. I do have one policy, and that is to conceal what my policies are. Except for the one I've just revealed. Damn. Now everyone knows."

The Tories were quick to attack Mr Blair for his admission that he had a no-policy policy. Said one leading Conservative: "We don't have any policies either. But in our case it is not a matter of policy. It is purely incompetence."

Mr Alastair Campbell is in the soup.

School news

St Cake's

Blair Term begins today. There are 367 boys in the school and 3 girls. V.A.T. Surcharge (Blunkett's) is Chief Taxer. Yu Turn (Prescott's) is Shadow Head Boy. Mr Klaus Four is on an extended sabbatical and his replacement has yet to be announced. Ms Mo Mowlam takes over as Chief Matron from Mrs Margaret Beckett. Skinners will be run over Cook's Beard on 2 March. There will be a performance of *The Hippopotamus* by Stephen Fry O.C., adapted for the stage by John Mortimer, in the Neil Kinnock Memorial Hall on 29 March. The School Orchestra will perform Mandelson's *A Midsummer Night's Dream of Winning the General Election*. The "Cake's Lecture" will be given in the Glenys Kinnock Women's Studies Block by Mr Richard Gott O.C. on "With Russia From Love". Omovs will be on 4 April.

QUENTIN TARANTEATIME

"Shall I be motherfucker?"

NICHOLAS

FLINTSTONE NEWS

20,000 BC, Friday   Price: 2 Tusks

NEW PAINTINGS DISAPPOINT

by Our Art Staff
Brian Pseudocriticus

A DISMAL new show has opened at the Cave Gallery in the Ardèche which once again highlights the paucity of the contemporary art scene.

Dull daubs in ochre and red with crude black outlines have been rendered directly onto the wall, with no thought for shape, design of composition — images are even superimposed one on top of the other.

The same dreary menagerie of mammoth, bison and tiger is trotted out by an artist rightly withholding his signature. There is nothing new here and we have seen it all before at Lascaux, Les Eyzies and all the other over-praised Dordogne caves.

How we yearn for the work of Van Gog, Rembrog, or Michaelangelog *(continued for centuries)*.

A Taxi Driver writes

Every week a well-known cab driver is asked to give his views on an issue of topical importance.

This week: Paul Nutter (Cab no. 666)

Blimey, he's hopeless, isn't he, guv? John Major? Don't make me laugh. Did you see that press conference? What did he think he was doing? Taking the piss, or what? My kiddy could have done better than that. Know what I think, guv? Best thing they can do is bring back Maggie. She'd soon sort them out. She was a proper leader, not like this one they've got in now. I tell you, mate. me and all the blokes on the rank reckon there's only one thing to do with him. String 'im up. It's the only language people like him understand.

I 'ad that Lord Keith Joseph in the back of the cab once. Now he was a real gent. Made a lot of sense too. Traffic's terrible, isn't it? You'd be quicker walking. That'll be fifteen quid.

(This cab driver appears by kind permission of the Daily Mail)

NEXT WEEK: Richard Littlejohnson.

Forward to 2000

by Our Environment Staff **Cecil B. de Millennium**

MILLIONS of suggestions have been pouring in to the office of Heritage Minister Stephen Drivel for imaginative ways in which Britain can mark the year 2000.

Dribble has already shortlisted ten of the top schemes which will make Britain the most exciting place in the world to be in when the clock strikes midnight on 31 December 1999.

Here are the ten projects to make the next 1000 years go off with a bang:

1. Giant Tibetan Prayer-Wheel made from recycled bottle tops, to be erected in the nave of Westminster Abbey.
2. Two billion trees to be planted in a straight line from John O'Groats to Land's End.
3. Red Arrows to fly through the Channel Tunnel in formation.
4. Covering Snowdonia with huge pizza designed by Damien Hirst.
5. 4,000ft-high hologram of the 12 stars of the European Union to be displayed over the Palace of Westminster.
6. The Three Tenors to sing *We'll*

Meet Again with Dame Vera Lynn, suspended in hot-air balloon over White Cliffs of Dover.

7. The making of the world's biggest ball of string, to be erected in the Pennines, visible from space.
8. Free HobNob biscuit to be issued to every old age pensioner on 1 January 2000.
9. The flooding of the Centre Court at Wimbledon in the presence of Her Majesty the Queen, to create a marine and aquatic arena for the re-enactment of famous naval battles from history.
10. Mr David Mellor to be ritually executed on Tower Hill by Mr Blobby, live on BBC-1.

If you have any suggestions as to how £10 billion from the National Lottery could be wasted on similar schemes, write at once to Stephen Grovel, Ministry of Heritage, London SW1 1AAARG.

STORM OVER BBC'S 'CLASSIC DRAMA' SHOCKER

by Our TV Staff
Edith Whartsonthetellytonight

HUNDREDS of angry Tory MPs have complained over the BBC's latest adaptation, this time a new version of Beatrix Potter's classic novel *Peter Rabbit*, for showing on BBC-1 next autumn.

The adapter, Ms Drearie Sludge, yesterday defended her decision to add scenes showing rape and homosexuality to the story, to make it "relevant to the twentieth century audience".

The Buccaneer Stops Here

In the new version of the well-loved Potter children's tale, retitled *Reservoir Rabbits*, the hero Peter, accompanied by his gay friend Benjamin, goes into the garden, where the happy-go-lucky pair indulge in an orgy of stealing and group sex, involving various mice, frogs and hedgehogs.

When an interfering grown-up, Mr MacGregor, tries to stop the action, Peter "blows him away" and the two return home to their mother.

Said BBC-1 controller Mr Alan Botney yesterday: "Every age retells the stories in its own language. Shakespeare did it with Plutarch, and so did Dickens.

"To suggest that we are just doing this in a desperate bid to get an audience is totally true."

Sir Marmaduke Hussey is 127.

"It's not a gun in my pocket — I'm pleased to see you"

41

Crème de la Crème Advertising

Major Television Company requires Director

Anglia Television is looking to replace a senior member of the Board. Applicants should be totally unknown and ideally not married to a famous novelist.

The applicant should not have access to a fax and should not have spoken to her husband for several years.

Salary negotiable (but does not include huge payoffs for Kurds, etc).

National Newspaper requires EDITOR

The Grauniad is looking for a new editor. Candidates should ideally not belong to the KGB or be in the habit of forging faxes from Members of Parliament. Anyone considered. Spelling not essential. *(Candidates with sense of humour need not apply.)*

GOOD KING SENSELESSNESS

RADIO FOUR

The Today Programme

John Humbug: …So, Jurgen Dirk, you're in charge of the Dutch emergency services. Do you think the dykes are going to hold? Or will the water break through, killing thousands of people?

Dirk: I think not, Mr Humbug. I am glad to say that the water has been going down.

Humbug: Oh. You mean there isn't going to be the worst disaster for 40 years with millions made homeless and massive loss of life?

Dirk: Well, no, at the moment we have everything under control. And…

Humbug: …well, that's disappointing. Not much of a story over there in Holland.

Anna Fraud: Well, at least someone's died here in England. The veal protester who was run over by a lorry. Mr Cedric Sandal, you're the organiser of BAAA, the Ban All Animal Abuse campaign. Don't you feel you are responsible for this woman's death?

Sandal: Er, well, no, it was a tragic accident. We're all very upset.

Fraud: So you're denying that you killed her. Then perhaps we should blame the police. Superintendent Knacker, you were in charge yesterday. Why didn't you stop this happening?

Knacker: It was a very tragic accident.

Fraud: Oh come on. A woman has just been killed. It's a big story. And surely it's your duty to help us string it out for a few more minutes. I mean, there should be regulations to stop this sort of thing happening.

Knacker: … er…

Fraud: Well, that's all we've got time for.

Humbug: And now, Thought For The Day, from the Rev. J.C. Flannel.

Flannel: I was originally going to talk about Eric Cantona. But then the Sikh man did that story yesterday. So then I listened to the news and thought "should it be the awful floods, or should it be the very important question of animal transportation." And then I realised that I could do both, by talking about the story of Noah. He knew what a flood was. And his only response was to herd animals in inhuman conditions in a floating wooden crate. Just imagine what it must have been like for all those poor animals, looking out with their sad eyes…

Humbug: …thank you, vicar. Now, let's see if we can really stir up some trouble in Northern Ireland, with this new leaked document showing that the British Government is planning to hand over Ulster to Dublin by the end of the year. Ian Paisley, there's going to be blood on the streets, isn't there…

(Contd. every morning on 94 kHz)

The Alternative Rocky Horror Service Book

No. 94. A Service Of Commination On The National Lottery

Bishop *(for it is he):* O Lord, who said "Whenever two or three are gathered together, they are likely to be queuing for a lottery ticket", deliver us from the temptation of £18 million.

All: Are you sure you meant that? You could do a lot with £18 million.

Bishop: O ye of little faith, I beseech ye to abjure the National Lottery and all its works. For it is an abomination unto the Lord, even though a proportion of the proceeds has been set aside for charitable and artistic purposes.

All: Like sick kiddies and the opera house.

Bishop: Very true. We will now sing the first verse of Cole Porter's stirring hymn, 'Who Wants To Be A Millionaire?'.

All: We do.

There will then be a reading from the Book of Numbers: "14-44-31-21-6-4."

All: And what is this week's bonus number?

Bishop: It is 13.

All: Damn. We've lost again. You are right. It is a real waste of money.

Bishop: Did I not tell you so?

At this point there shall be another reading, from the Epistle of Camelot to the Church of England.

Dear Bishop:
Do you want some money to mend your roof? Support the lottery and it could be you!

Bishop: Alright, you win. Tickets will be on sale in the vestry after this service.

THE DISMISSAL

Bishop: Depart in hope.

All: Thanks be to greed.

© Carealot plc

Pass Notes

No 94: Alan Rubbisher

Occupation: New editor of the Guardian.

Appearance: Bespectacled schoolboy. 17 going on 58.

So why him? Good question.

No why, really? Ask me another.

Is he a member of the KGB: No. He's a member of the Garrick.

Not to be confused with: MI5 man James Rusbridger, of fatal auto-erotic accident fame.

But didn't he write a book about sex manuals? No. That was Alan Rusbridger, the new editor of the Guardian.

So what changes can we expect? The Guardian is going to be more reader-friendly.

You mean they're going to fire Ed Pearce and Suzanne Moore… No. He likes them.

So what are his politics? Soft-left. Soft-right. Soft-porn.

You mean: He likes to get tits and bums in between the dreary bits about social workers.

Most likely to say: Let's get Claudia Schiffer on the cover and do a piece about exploitation of women by the media.

Least likely to say: I only got this job because I invented Pass Notes.

Peter McLie

The World's Worst Columnist*

WILL Camilla ever divorce her husband? I doubt it. Many married couples manage to live separate lives without too much fuss. So why not Camilla and her soldier-husband? Indeed, I would go so far as to bet that these two sensible people will be together well into the next century! Isn't marriage grandy and dandy?!

YOU DON'T see much of David Attenborough on the TV these days do you? Personally I always enjoyed his *Animal Magic* programmes. But I reckon it's time he changed his tack and turned his gaze to the fascinating world of plants. And here's a title for his new series — Coronation Street.

*apart from Norman Tebbit

LAST QUANGO IN PARIS

'FEWER TRAINS WILL MEAN BETTER SERVICE' says Government

by Our Privatisation Staff
N.M. Rothschild

THE Transport Minister Mr Brian Morelooney yesterday explained how rail privatisation would bring a vastly improved service for Britain's rail customers.

He announced that the new franchise holders would have to run a minimum number of trains.

"In some cases this number could even be as high as one train per day," he claimed.

Great Train Robbery

"By concentrating on providing the best possible service once a day," Mr Morelooney explained, "it will be possible for the operators to ensure that every train is entirely full.

"Also," he went on, "safety would be greatly improved, since there will be no risk of collision when there are no other trains competing for trackspace.

"Passengers sitting on the roof or clinging to the sides will be issued with special safety instructions to ensure that when the train is approaching a tunnel they jump off and continue their journey on foot."

Just The Ticket

Another increase in efficiency will be the reduction of core ticket sales outlets from the present 3,000 to just one, based in Aberdeen Parkway.

Customers who wish to buy through-tickets to any station on the new privatised network will be able to drive to pick up their ticket in no more than eight hours.

Said Mr Morelooney: "All this will result in a leaner and more non-existent rail service. The benefits will be obvious. Train strikes will be a thing of the past — as will the trains."

"We don't say that Ronnie is too thick to go to college, we say that he's University Challenged..."

Valentine Greetings from the Blairs

Happy Darling?

It's too early to say

Roses are red.
Violets are blue.
So are the Tories,
But Labour are too.
Vote for me.

Poetry Corner

So. Farewell then
Me.

I was sent
Off.

I was so angry
I could have kicked myself.

Instead
I kicked a fan.

E.J. Cantona (Poet and Footballer)

NEW WORDS

HOWARD

n. rhyming slang for man too scared to resign. One who is shifty, evasive, appears on television far too often. Example: "In my day a howard like that would have been shot at dawn". (W. Deedesh *Somme Like It Hot* 1914.)

LEWIS

n. synonym for howard (see above). Shifty little man who refuses to take responsibility for fear of losing performance related bonus. Example: "Did you see that lewis on the telly again last night? A case of arrant howardice if ever I saw one". (Overheard in pub 1995.)

ILLINGWORTH

n. a measure of rich humbug, prob. originating in Yorkshire. Used figuratively of person who claims credit for success but blames others for failure. Examples: any interview with Chairman of England's cricket selectors. (See 'fletcher' below).

FLETCHER

n. slang, originating in Essex. Southern version of illingworth (above). Used figuratively of person who is quick to blame others for failure, but immediately claims credit for success. Examples: any interview with manager of England cricket team.

MAJOR

n. (obscure) political version of a howard, a lewis, an illingworth or a fletcher, except worse.

ROTHSCHILD

n. form of tip or rubbish heap on which unwanted items are placed. Now often used figuratively of the employers of superannuated politicians. Example: "He was so useless they had to throw him on the rothschild." (*Tales of Wakeham or Mr Lamont's Lucky Break* by A. Trollope)

CANTONA

n. fashionable cant or humbug, purveyed by large number of people, esp. hack journalists. Example: "Did you see that load of cantona in the Guardian this morning, or was it the Mail?" (Overheard in all pubs, January 1995)

(That's enough words, Ed.)

ANNOUNCEMENT

The artist hitherto known as Prince wishes it to be known that in future he wants to be called Charles. Charles feels that the title 'Prince' no longer suits him since it is perfectly clear that he is never going to be King.

$$E = mc^2$$

"One has to make allowances for genius"

THE DAILY TELEGRAPH

NOTEBOOK

VICTORIA COREN

WELL I never. A vicar on *Blind Date*! Whatever will they think of next? Probably a vicar on *Blind Date*!

☐ MY flatmate at college used to have an Athena poster up on her wall.

And now Athena have gone bust.

Blimey!

☐ OOH-AAH Cantona. He's just amazing, right?

And anyone who says he isn't must be mad.

It's like when your parents tell you off for smoking in your bedroom.

What are we meant to do, for God's sake?

Play football?

☐ I HAD to wait half an hour for the bus today. And then, would you believe it, three came along at once.

Have you noticed how often that happens?

When I told my Dad, he said: "I could make a column out of that."

So I did!

Whatever next? A vicar on *Blind Date*?

ON OTHER PAGES

☐ Should Nigella Lawson be smacked for writing self-righteous rubbish about child care in The Times? asks everybody.

Woman claims £200 million after swallowing fly

by Our Legal Staff **Roger Law and Peter Carter Fluck**

AN ELDERLY woman is to sue the government after swallowing a fly which, she claims, led to her suffering from the effects of PFSTS, or "post-fly-swallowing trauma syndrome".

Following a recent ruling of the European Fairy Tale Court, the woman, whose name is not being revealed, is entitled to sue the government for failing to protect her from the harmful effects of fly-swallowing.

One Swallow Makes £200 Million

A leading doctor, who is to appear on behalf of the unnamed woman, described how, as a result of swallowing the fly, his patient had been driven by a compulsion to swallow a succession of increasingly large creatures, culminating in a horse. "She is now very dangerously ill," he said, "through no fault of her own. My prognosis is that she may soon be dead."

Lawyers are keenly watching the outcome of the so-called "fly case", as it could well set a historic precedent which would enable them to earn huge sums of money *(shurely 'to help other victims of injustice'? Ed)*.

The London firm of Feigh & Pay have a number of other cases pending. These include:

● A Miss Muffet, who suffered from Spider-Induced Stress (SIS) after a large arachnid sat down beside her while she was relaxing on a tuffet.

● An unnamed cat which was "severely traumatised" by the experience of being put in a well by a boy called Johnny Green, before being rescued by Thomas Stout. The cat, which is suing the local authority that owns the well, claims that it was "disoriented" by the experience and is now "unable to catch mice or purr".

● The parents of a baby who left it unattended on the top of a tree are to sue the tree's owners after a bough broke, precipitating the infant to the ground, cradle and all.

RUDOLF VALENTARANTINO

"Fucking marry me, you fucking bitch"

THE ALTERNATIVE VOICE

This week **Dave Spart**, Co-Chair of the Death To Veal Farmers Peace Movement, writes about animal welfare.

Er... the martyrdom of that woman the other day murdered by the police in a totally cynical and calculated manner proves once and for all that there is no alternative to violent protest against the capitalist farming establishment led by arch-fascist William Waldegrave the Goebbels of the Veal Death Squads with his vast estates filled with helpless suffering veal who are sent to their deaths in order to line the pockets of the multinational Veal Barons who are propping up the reactionary dictatorship of Thatcher Reagan Major and the rest of the agro-military complex... er... and the press has typically notably and cynically ignored these legitimate protests in which ordinary people have united in their millions to show solidarity with their fellow veal many of whom are dying in their crates as they are held up at ports by protestors throwing stones and falling under lorries... er... er...

(contd page 94)

The Alternative Rocky Horror Service Book

No. 94. Service For The Rehabilitation of An Homosexual Playwright

The Dean *(for it is she)*: Brothers and sisters and celebrities. We are gathered here, under the eyes of the television cameras, to give thanks for the incomparable genius that was N— or M—. (Here he may say 'the divine Oscar', 'Noel' or 'Stephen Fry' when he goes.) There is only one thing worse than coming to Church.

All: And that is not coming to Church.

(Here the congregation may laugh)

Dean: No one speaks badly of Poets' Corner.

All: Only those that cannot get into it do that.

(Here the congregation may roll in the aisles)

The Dean: Oscar is to be commemorated in a window.

All: A *window*?

Dean: And where is this window to be placed?

All: In the south transept.

Dean: Ah, the unfashionable side! There shall then be a reading from N— or M— (here the Dean may introduce some leading thespian, such as Dame Judi Dench or Sir Ian McKellen).

Celeb: The reading is taken from the Holy Bible.

All: One should always have something sensational to read in church.

(Here various elderly actors may have to be resuscitated following an attack of hysterical amusement)

Celeb: *The Book of Oscar* Chapter One.

1. And, lo, there was one whose name was Oscar, who spake in paradox.

2. But he was betrayed by his friend, which was called Bo-sey.

3. And he was crucified by the British Establishment.

4. And they took him to the place which is called Reading. And there he was cast into outer darkness.

5. But after a hundred years had passed he rose again, and was put into a window. Here endeth the Reading Gaol.

"You'll never get in, My Liege. That castle is impregnable"

All: That's very good. We wish we'd thought of that.

Dean: You will, brethren, you will. After the final hymn, you are all invited to the Café Royal for lukewarm champagne and stale crisps.

All: Ah, so we will be the unspeakable in pursuit of the uneatable!

Hymn: *He's Got The Whole World In His Handbag* (Words: St Matthew Parris. Tune: Mary Wesley).

© Carey & Sharey Productions 1995.

CABINET UNITED

Robbie Burns' Traditional Lament on the Death of Sir Nicholas Fairbairn MP

Gang awa' wi ye,
Ya cream-faced loon.
Wi yer tartan trews
And yer boozy breath.

Wi yer hands
A-wanderin' o'er the wee
    young lassies.
They'll no be saddened
By yer untimely death.

© Rabbie Lionel Burns

SHOULD BRITAIN BE ALLOWED TO TAKE PART IN VE-DAY CELEBRATIONS

by Our Euro-Staff
Ray D. O'Luxembourg

MEPs were last night considering the controversial question of what part, if any, Britain should be allowed to play in this year's celebrations of the 50th anniversary of Victory for Europe Day.

"The perpetrators of the infamous Crimes of Dresden and, er, Dresden, have no place alongside all those brave Germans and Frenchmen who did so much to rid Europe of the Nazi menace," said one MEP, Herr Grossdeutsch.

British MEPs said that "we should respect the feelings of our European partners on this very sensitive issue. It is too early to expect the Germans to forgive us for having declared war on them in 1939."

Lord Howe-Howe is 86.

"It's a lovely day, Elmer. Let's go kill an abortionist"

The RAF — Then and Now

1945

Hoorah for the Allies!

Let's carpet-bomb Dresden!

There'll be a firestorm!

'Bomber' Harris

1995

Hoorah for Allied!

Let's carpet my house!

There'll be a storm and you'll get fired!

Sir Sandy Wilson

LEGENDARY romantic comedy charting the 'rites of passage' of a shy young non-graduate about to embark on a career in cement garden-gnome manufacture.

When he meets Mrs Kierans, the experienced, alluring older woman from across the road, his whole world is turned upside down. The sexy divorcée initiates the amazed young John into all the delights of love in the afternoon — and in return John teaches her how to eat fish and chips out of a newspaper.

But John's mother does not approve. When they go on holiday to the Costa Brava, she insists on coming too — and sleeping between them in the bed.

It's no wonder poor John went mad and became prime minister.

Watch out for the classic scene where Mrs Robinson *(shurely 'Kierans'? Ed)* takes off her Winceyette nightie to the strains of John's favourite song, *Bridge Over Troubled Waterloo Station*. But John says: "No thank you, Mrs Kierans. In my judgement any hanky-panky might not inconsiderably damage my political career."

The Non-Graduate

Cast in Full

JOHN MAJOR	. . . .	Norman Wisdom	TERRY MAJOR-BALL	Eric Morecambe
MRS KIERANS	. . . .	Anne Bancroft	NORMA JOHNSON	Julie Andrews
MRS MAJOR	. . . .	Irene Handl	MAN IN PUB	Terry-Thomas

Directed by Bryan Forbes

DRESDEN BLITZED BY MASS APOLOGIES

by Our Wartime Staff **Sir Osbert Lancaster-Bomber-Harris**

THE HISTORIC city of Dresden today vanished beneath an unprecedented barrage of apologies, delivered by an armada of English clergymen and members of the Royal Family.

The sky was black with Lufthansa planes flying in over the ruined Saxon capital, packed with bishops and senior servicemen eager to say "it was all our fault".

Said wartime historian Max Hitler *(contd p. 94)*

"Apparently the bloke next door is an old Bond villain"

BIGGEARS FLIES AGAIN

by CAPT. W.E. JOHNS

"THAT looks a lark," said Group Captain 'Biggears' Windsor, more formally known as His Royal Highness the Prince of Wales. "Can I have a bash at landing the old crate?"

His co-pilot, Squadron Leader "Ginger" Gingerson, looked worried.

"Are you sure you know what you're doing, Sir?"

"Of course I do. I'm the heir to the throne. Now give me the bally joystick."

"Very well, Your Majesty."

The plane took a sickening dive and screamed towards the runway. There was a sound of rending metal, squealing rubber and screaming sheep as the BAE-146 Feeder Jet flopped onto the tarmac.

"Cripes! Biggears! You've pranged the kite!" shouted a shaken Ginger as the £30 million aircraft ploughed into the thick peat bog of Islay.

"Don't worry. Everything's under control," announced Biggears cheerfully.

"What do you mean 'under control'?" stammered Ginger as the stricken turbo-jet sank slowly into the Scottish mud.

"Well, there will be an official enquiry, and *you* will take all the blame.

"And you, Sir?"

"I'll get off scot-free and then tell everyone I'm too busy to fly any more."

"Hoorah, Sire!" cried the disgraced ex-Squadron Leader. "Biggears lies again!"

© *Boy's Own.*

STORM GROWS OVER 'OBSCENE' £1 MILLION PAY SHOCKER

by Our Business Staff
Sir Peter Paybotham

A HUGE ROW erupted last night after it was leaked that a former public service utility had agreed to pay out a "telephone number" salary-and-benefits package to one of their senior executives.

He is Sir Christopher Evans, 26, formerly head of Toothbrush plc, and before that one of the founders of the Big Breakfast media/leisure conglomerate.

Sir Christopher is to be paid £350,000 a year to act as part-time chairman of BBC Radio One's *Good Morning* show.

Good Evans

Defending the BBC's decision to pay Evans £2,000-a-minute, Mr Matthew Bannister, Chief Executive of the BBC's Remuneration Unit (Radio One), said angrily: "Sir Christopher is worth every penny. He is extremely hard working. He gets up very early. And he has an unrivalled knowledge of the breakfast radio industry.

"These days," Mr Bannister went on, "the intensively competitive international disc jockey market dictates that the best corporate talent will follow the highest available remuneration on a global basis.

"If the BBC had not snapped up Sir Christopher's services at a remarkably reasonable rate, he could well have been headhunted for a twelve-figure salary by Radio Milwaukee's *Good Morning Milwaukee* show.

"When you think that he is only getting the same salary as some jumped-up little bureaucrat running North-West Water, you realise what a stupid world we are living in."

"Extra! Extra! Mind your own business!"

'Elitist' programmes to go in Birt's £2 billion shake-up

IN THE most radical shake-up of the BBC since last year, Director-General John Birt has decided to implement his £100 million Programme Review.

Out go such elitist BBC programmes as:
- EastEnders
- The National Lottery Show
- Noel's House Party
- Match of the Day
- Neighbours
- EastEnders Omnibus

Islamic Baywatch

In come a whole new range of programmes specially designed to appeal to the majority of people in Britain, i.e. all the minorities.
- Inspector Hatterjee Investigates
- Leroy's House Party
- Highlights of the Chinese Women's Football League
- Biro Collecting Today, with Christos Christodoulos and Ranjat Panjay.
- The Not Getting Up Show — a youth special targeted at the 14-17 year-olds who don't want to get out of bed, even to watch television.
- The Private Life of Toast, a 14-part series for Britain's toast-loving minority, with Cliff Michelmore amd Mbutu Onanugu.
- Plus more programmes for East Anglians, Red Indians, Red Ken, High Street Ken, grapefruit segments and others. *(Viewers switch over to ITV as usual.)*

Who do YOU want to present the BBC News and Current Affairs?

No	YES
Jeremy Paxman	Jeremy Beadle
Richard Baker	Danny Baker
Sue Cameron	Su Pollard
Jim Naughtie	Jimmy Greaves
John Humphries	John Inman (Mr Humphries from *Are You Being Served?*)

(That's enough — Ed.)

A Taxi Driver writes

For the first time ever, an Irish cab driver is invited to comment on an issue of topical importance.

This week: **Seamus O'Littlejohn** (Cab No. 3) on the violence at the Ireland England Football Match.

See those English yobboes? They're all the same, the English. All they want is the drinkin' and the fightin'. Always been the same. Lazy, good-for-nothing boyos, just lookin' for trouble. There'll never be any solution to the English problem, I'm tellin' you. I'd stop them comin' over here. They should cut the island of Britain adrift and let it float out into the Atlantic. It's the only language these English understand. I had that Henry Kelly in the back of the cab once. A proper English gentleman he was, and no mistake.
NEXT WEEK: Seamus Heaney (Cab No. 7) on Post-Wildean Irony.

"You should try and take things easier Mr Blue-Arse"

Rhymes For Today

They seek him here, they seek him there
They seek that Stephen Fry everywhere.
Is he in France, or is he in Bruges?
Who gives a toss?

Adapted from the original Hungarian by Simon Gray.

MAKE YOUR OWN CLAUSE FOUR

A Private Eye Cut Out 'n' Keep Service

Now is your chance to redefine Socialism in the comfort and privacy of your own home.

All you have to do is to cut out these key words, arrange them in the order of your choice and — hey presto! — you're Tony Blair!

Those words:

opportunity
democratic
commitment
training
potential
mixed
economy
leopardskin
social
accessories
gender
goal
equality
justice

Send to Mr Jonathan Prescott, Word Processor House, London SW94P 1LP or email gobbledegook@walworth.org.uk

---

'NO ONE TO BLAME'
says Bank of England enquiry

by Our Barings Staff **Lunchtime O'Nol'mbroke**

MR Edward "Eddie" George, the Governor of the Bank of England, yesterday published a full and frank enquiry into the conduct of the Bank of England during the collapse of the Barings merchant bank.

The one-page document exonerates Mr George of any responsibility at all for anything that happened at any time.

The report concludes with a ten-point resumé of Mr George's key findings about himself.

1. The Bank of England was not aware of anything at any stage, which is its job as regulator.

2. Even if it *had* **been aware of anything, it could not have acted in any way to prevent the collapse of a major bank because that is not its function as a financial watchdog.**

3. Mr George was anyway on holiday at the time, skiing in the Austrian ski resort of Schloss Apacket.

7. Mr George had it on the personal authority of his very old friend Mr Peter Baring that it was all the fault of "some oik".

29. Since nothing untoward has happened, it will obviously never happen again.

37. Your money is safe with us.

574. Er…

1028. That's it.

GO TO FUCKING SLEEP, YOU FUCKING FUCK!

OVALTARANTINO

JOHN BYRNE

52

Those Borings in full

What are they like, the colourful dynasty who have run Britain's oldest banking empire for thousands of years?

Sir Peter Boring, 57. Tight-lipped supremo of Boring Bros, the family bank. When asked yesterday what he thought about losing all the family's money and presiding over the downfall of the Queen's bank, he said: "Good evening."

Lady Sexilia Boring, 21. Supermodel 7th cousin of Sir Cedric

Boring, the last governor of Tanganyika. Once appeared in the Peterborough column when she was mistaken for her cousin, Lady Drusilla Boring *(see below)*.

Lord Basingstoke, 65. Reclusive former head of Boring Charitable Trust, when, as the Hon. Archie Boring, he awarded an annual grant of

£500 to the New Dworkin Contraceptive Dance Troupe.

Lady Rose Kennedy Boring, 109.

Formerly the Keeper of the Queen's Hot Water Bottle. Matriarch of the clan, she remains hugely powerful, although dead.

Hon. Paddington Baring, 20. Sacked from Eton for arriving at a London railway terminus without a ticket.

Nick Leeson, 25. Council-house born cause of the downfall of

all the above. When asked why he had hired Mr Fivers to run his Far East derivatives operation, Sir Peter Boring said: "Good evening."

LEESON INNOCENT

I was only placing very large orders

TRADING BEGINS IN LEESON FUTURES

4 years!

5 years!

50 lashes!

Double it!

EXPERT ANALYSIS

Our City Editor answers your questions

Q. What exactly is a derivative?

A. A derivative is a very complex financial instrument. Put simply, it is the dealer's way of er... um... it's a sort of gambling, yes, that's it, gambling, whereby the trader bets, as it were, on er... er... look at it another way. You know the Nikkei Index? The one that is a bit like the Hang Seng and the Footsie? Well, that goes up and down and er... er... I'll start again. You know that bit in *Wall Street* where the guy in the braces shouts "I'm long on pork bellies"? No, sorry, that was *Trading Places*... er... er... as I said it's basically stocks and shares, buying and selling, gilts futures, up three points, down three points, that sort of thing, OK? Er... er... suffice to say that getting involved with Derivatives is very risky indeed. You get in deeper than you think, you don't know what you're doing, you try and cover it up and you end up thoroughly discredited, probably losing your job and having to run away.

Q. Where are you going with that suitcase?

A. Bye!

© All newspapers

HOLLYWOOD
An Apology

IN COMMON with all other newspapers we may in recent weeks have given the impression that the forthcoming 1995 Oscar Awards Ceremony was the cultural highlight of the year, on the grounds that all the top prizes were expected to go to the greatest films ever made, i.e. *The Madness of Eddie George* and *Four Weddings and Liz Hurley*. **Headlines such as "The Brits Are Coming", "Hollywood Says British Is Best" and "Is *Yes Minister* Man Gay?" may have led readers to believe that the Academy of Motion Picture judges were an extraordinarily important and discerning group of persons.**

We now realise, in the light of the decision by these thick, vulgar Yankee dimwits to give 84 awards to such a worthless glorification of schmaltzy stupidity as *Forrest Gump*, that the Oscar ceremony is nothing more than an empty, self-regarding charade which exposes Hollywood as merely a parochial tinseltown devoid of any critical faculties and revealing America itself to be nothing more than a colossal black hole of vacuity imploding into its own bottomless pit of narcissism.

We apologise for any confusion which may have arisen on this point.

© All newspapers.

Bishop admits relationship with God

by Our Religious Affairs Correspondent **Clifford Longford**

THE Church of England was cast into further turmoil today when a senior Bishop confessed that he had enjoyed what he called "a close relationship" with God for many years.

"Yes," he said. "I am a practising Christian and have been for a long time. I got into this habit when I was a young priest and have successfully covered it up in order to advance in my career."

The bishop then admitted that he talked to God on a regular basis, sometimes up to three or four times a day.

"I have always been ashamed of this," he explained, "and now I have decided to retire and take up a more suitable job."

For legal reasons the bishop cannot be named. He is the Right Reverend Robin Goodfellow, Suffragan Bishop of Bishop Auckland.

That St Patrick's Day procession in full

Start at O'Malley's Genuine Auld Ireland Pizza Parlour East 417th Street, New York.

1st Float
(in shape of Giant Shamrock)
St Gerald of Adams shaking hands with President Clintstone.

1st, 2nd, 3rd and 4th
Security Vehicles
with men in sunglasses running alongside.

2nd Float
(in shape of Giant Armalite Rifle)
Mr M. McGuinness surrounded by armed members of the Sinn Fein peace movement.

1st Band Fife and
Drum John Majorettes
Led by Paddy O'Mayhew, playing a medley of traditional Irish airs, including *Cock-Ups And Mussels, Never On Bloody Sunday* and *When Irish IRAs Are Smiling.*

The Massed Noraid Tin Rattlers
Led by New York's own Master Tin Rattler Tip O'Rarey collecting "Dollars For Peace" from the crowd.

1st Episcopal Stretch-Limousine
Cardinal Archbishop Shameless O'Gunrunner, Archbishop of Armalite, accompanied by his Chaplain Father O'Lovechild.

3rd Float
(in shape of Giant TV Studio)
A cross-section of Irish-American celebrities, including Mickey Rourke, Mickey Rooney, Mickey O'Mouse, Mike O'Tyson, and the late J.F. Kennedy, accompanied by Sister Whoopee O'Goldberg.

Other Floats
There then followed a number of floats dedicated to the Irish-American Gay and Lesbian Republican Community (Ms Mollie O'Spart and friend). *(That's enough parade. Ed)*

"They're very Moorish, aren't they?"

ARCHBISHOP BLAIREY BATTLES FOR NEW CREED TO 'MOVE C of E INTO 21ST CENTURY'

by Our Religious Staff
Rabbi Lionel Blair

IN A DARING move to bring the Church of England into line with "the needs and aspirations of 1990s Britain", the Archbishop of Canterbury Dr George Blairey has decided to scrap the outdated Apostle's Creed.

"This mission statement," he said, "was written at a very different time more than 1500 years ago. It is no longer relevant to the modern world."

The Wondrous Cross-head

Blairey claims that "the spirit of the old creed will be maintained, although specific phrases will be dropped if they are deemed to be incompatible with the changing values of Britain's new pluralist society".

Out go "the communion of saints", "the forgiveness of sins" and any reference to the resurrection.

In come "the importance of inter-personal relationships", "toleration towards those of varied sexual orientation" and "opposition to the exporting of live veal calves."

In addition Bishop Blairey has appointed a team of media consultants, the firm of Hargleby, Gargleby and Beelzebub, to mount an "Easter offensive" on the nation's advertising hoardings, designed to woo the millions of potential consumers back into a "worship environment".

Among the mould-breaking poster designs the team has come up with are:

TAKE CARE!
C of E

HAVE A NICE DAY!
C of E

GOOD EVENING!
C of E

VOTE CONSERVATIVE!
C of E

Old Sayings

*Sky at night
No one's watching.*

"And bishops can go both ways, as long as they keep quiet about it"

Reevo..

An Open Letter to Mr Peter Tatchell from BlackRage!, the armed wing of the National Association of Blackmailers (NAB)

Dear Peter,

This letter is written in a spirit of loving hatred from a group of blackmailers who have had the courage to come out and admit to their blackmailness.

We have evidence in our possession that you, Peter Tatchell, are one of us, i.e. a practising blackmailer. And yet you consistently deny this when you appear in the media, e.g. the *Today* programme (on which, incidentally, you were pathetic).

We have no intention of giving this evidence to the tabloid press.

However you should remember that there are a lot of blackmailers out there who have to suffer prejudice, discrimination and blackmailophobia because people in the public eye like you fail to set an example by coming out honestly and admitting where your true inclinations lie — i.e. approaching other men and threatening to expose them. Unless we hear within 24 hours that you have openly declared yourself as a blackmailer, we shall have no alternative but to present the information we have to the tabloids, i.e. the Daily Blackmail.

Signed

a friend

55

GLENDA SLAGG

⭐ The Terror of the Tabloids ⭐

GOOD riddance to Ronnie Kray, the monster whose idea of a fun night out was to shoot someone in the head!!?!

I say Ronnie was scum from his bloodstained boots to his brylcreemed bonce!?!

So he died a miserable death from smoking 140 fags a day!! Pity it wasn't 240 — then he would have left us sooner!!?

That's Glenda's verdict on this vermin of vice!!?

SHED a tear for big-hearted Ronnie Kray!?!

All right, so he was a bit of a psychopath and a killer!?!

But dear old Ronnie loved his Mum and never touched a toddler!?!

When Ronnie ruled the East End you could walk safely down to your local pub and get shot!?!

You can't do that now, Mister!?!!

HAVE you read the new Martin Amis??

Nor have I!!!

Clear off sunshine, with your 500 grand and your fancy dental work and give us a break!?!!

Who do they think they are, these swarthy Don Pedros with their sombreros and castanets a-crawlin' and a-trawlin' where they don't belong!?!

Get back to tormenting bulls, amigos, and leave our poor lil 'ole hake and halibut alone!?!!

Byeeeeee!

HERE they are, Glenda's Mad March Machos;

RUPERT PENNANT-RAE. He's the deputy governor of the BONK of England! Geddit??!?

CHRIS EUBANK. I'll go a few rounds with you any night of the week! Ewhunk!!! (Geddit???)

DON JAIME DE MANICHARLAR Y SAENZ DE TEJADA — crazy name, crazy guy!?!!

STOP PRESS:

So the Spanish fishermen are trying to get their hands on our Canadian cousins' fish!!?!?

Doesn't it make you sick!??! (And I don't mean the fish, mister!?!)

YES! IT'S OUT!

VIDEO LATEST

They said it would never be released! Now at last

FOUR MURDERS AND A FUNERAL

Old fashioned British comedy of the type you hoped you would never see again! The story of the shy, diffident, archetypal Englishman and his refusal to get married due to the fact that he was a psychopathic homosexual. Includes hit Auden poem:

"His sexuality was a Kray area" N. de Jongh, the *Evening Standard*.

So. Farewell Then. Ron.

We do not Know where you Have gone.

Is it heaven Or is It hell? (We can guess. Ed)

© The Estate of the late E.J. Auden.

"Oh, come on, Henry. Three curtain calls is enough"

THE STATE FUNERAL OF MR RONALD KRAY
A Nation Mourns
Live from the Bethnal Green Crematorium

David Dimblebore: ...and so here, in the heart of London's colourful East End, they have come in their millions to pay their last respects to the greatest Englishman of them all as he comes home to his last resting place through the streets which he loved.

Along the pavements they stand with bowed heads, occasionally wiping away a silent tear as they await the cortege of the man they knew as "The Guv'nor".

And here now at last comes the procession. At the front, in the black Rover 2000 with its headlights dipped in homage, Inspector "Knacker of the Yard" Knacker, whose arrest of Ronnie on that March day of 1969 was the greatest moment of his career.

Then behind him the hearse itself, drawn by six black horses of the Royal Housebreakers Cavalry, with their plumes reversed, carrying the mortal remains of gangland's greatest hero.

I can see the inscriptions on some of the wreaths now — "Good Riddance, From Your Mates In G-Wing", "May You Rot In Hell, Ronnie, From Mrs Jack The Hat" and "Goodbye Sailor, From All Your Friends In The Gay And Lesbian Community".

And then, with full armed prison escort, the dead man's brother Reginald, in his camelhair straitjacket, his monogrammed silver handcuffs glinting in the sun.

Comforting him by his side the much-loved figure of that grand old national

institution, Dame Barbara Windsor. We all, of course, remember her in great films such as *Carry On Up Your Knickers* and... er... There she is now, waving to the crowd and graciously signing autographs, her familiar giggle breaking the sombre hush of the crowd. And now the procession is just passing the scene of one of Ronnie's greatest victories, The Blind Beggar pub, where all those years ago he thrilled a nation by shooting Sid "The Weasel" Driberg 14 times in the head, because Sid had asked him for a light.

And there behind, marching with their heads held high, some of the greatest names in Britain's underworld legend. I can see Harry "Razors" Phibbs, Chris "The Spiv" Silvester, Rory "The Knight" Bruce and Charlie "Gorbals" Wilson, his face still bearing the proud scars of his famous run-in with Billy "The Book" Rees-Mogg.

What memories they must have between them, these proud old veterans. They are looking older now, some of them having difficulty walking without their kneecaps. They know they will not see Ronnie's like again. At the coming out of the Sun they will remember him, on pages 1, 2, 3, 7, 9, 11 and 94.

And, yes, now, above us, in the clear blue March sky, the ceremonial flypast by the helicopter of Scotland Yard's traffic control division, keeping an eye out no doubt for any stolen vehicles which may be joining the cortege.

Oh, and there — one, two, three, four — the sound of the 21 Sawn-Off Shotgun Salute, which has only been accorded to the very greatest figures in our island's proud criminal history.

And now I hand you over to Anna Ford, who is waiting inside the Church of the Blessed Myra Hindley, where Cardinal Sin is waiting to pay his own tribute to the life and work of St Ronald of Kray... Over to you, Anna.

(Sound of middle-class woman being mugged)

Voice: Give us the bag, right, and don't say nuffink.

Nick Ross *(for it is he):* And remember, sleep tight and don't have nightmares. Goodnight.

57

THAT PRINCE CHARLES SPEECH IN FULL

by Our Royal Staff Antonia Holden-Guest

"LADIES and gentlemen. I do think it's rather important that we stop running ourselves down as a nation, picking holes in everyone and being cynical and so forth. There is only one word for it. Appalling. I think people should show more respect to a person who is actually, you know, trying to do something positive, rather than just sneering at one and going on about one's private life. It's time we recovered our respect for the institutions that have made this country great. I am thinking, for instance, of the monarchy, which has been built up for hundreds of years. It would be so easy, ladies and gentlemen, to throw all this away, just because one person goes around appearing on television talking about his extra-marital, er, you know, thingies. And there's another great institution which I think we are in danger of taking too lightly. I mean marriage. I often think that we could learn a lot from the great culture of Islam, which teaches that a chap can have a lot of wives, so if he doesn't like one he can go off with someone else's. And another very good idea these chaps have is the *fatwa*. I wonder if we could have one, for instance, against Diana..."

THE TODAY PROGRAMME

John Humphrys: The question of bias at the BBC has been the lead story of the week, and this morning in the studio to discuss some of the issues raised by Conservative politicians we have... myself. Mr Humphrys, can I begin by...

John Humphrys: Could I make one thing clear before this discussion goes any further...

Humphrys: I'm sorry but I do think we are entitled to an answer, so if you'll let me put the question...

Humphrys: Certainly.

Humphrys: Are you or are you not guilty of bias?

Humphrys: Before I answer that, let me explain how a Today interviewer, like myself...

Humphrys: That's all very well, Mr Humphrys, but we only have limited time. So can I just put the question to you again...

Humphrys: I'm sorry, John, but I must be allowed to finish what I was saying.

Humphrys: Yes or no, it's all we have time for, because time is running out, and we really must get this point clear. Can I put it to you once again, in the very limited time we have left, are you a bit of a leftie?

Humphrys: How dare you impugn the integrity of a professional broadcaster with years of experience? I demand an apology...

Humphrys: So do I *(long silence).*

Sue MacGregor: Well, I'm afraid I'll have to cut you off there, because it's now 8.45 and time for Thought for the Day. Today's speaker is the Chief Druid...

Druid: Good morning, Brian, good morning Sue. Once again fish are in the news, and they seem to be causing a great deal of trouble. As my dear old granny used to say...

(Contd. 94.3KHz)

N.U.T. STRIKE THREAT

How will we know, sir?

"We've isolated the gene that causes My Little Pony..."

LOTTERY LOSER TO SUE

by Our Legal Staff
TV's Joshua Rozenbeard

A 42-year-old milkman from Newport Pagnell is to sue the Heritage Minister, alleging "traumatic stress disorder" following his failure to win last week's £27 million National Lottery jackpot.

Said father of three Phil Float, who asked to remain anonymous: "I could not believe it when the numbers came up and mine were nothing like them.

"Ever since then my life has been a misery. I cannot sleep and I cannot concentrate on anything for more than a few minutes."

Instant Whinge

Mr Float claimed that he could no longer deliver milk to the correct houses and had been threatened with the sack by his employers, Pagnell Milk Services plc ("We Deliver. You drink.").

Mr Float is asking for compensation in the region of £27 million.

"The Government must step in and give me a lot of money for nothing."

OLD DOG REPRIEVED SHOCK

THE EUROPEAN Court today granted an 11th hour reprieve to the 54-year-old Complete Bull Terrier, known as "Dempstey", after its owner Lord Rothermere proved that "it did not represent a threat to anyone".

A tearful Lord Rothermere had been told to put Dempstey down on the grounds that he might attack an unknown actress or a very obscure member of the Royal Family.

"My Dempstey is not like that," said Rothermere. "He has no teeth at all and anyway he is always kept muzzled. He would not harm a fly. I take him everywhere I go and all my friends love old Dempstey. When he sees my rich mates he wags his tail and then licks their arses in an affectionate manner.

Lap Dog

"He is not a dangerous Bull Terrier as he has been telling everyone. He is a pet poodle."

Ivana Trump is grateful.

Reprinted from *The New Yorker*

WOEBEGONE DAYS

by GARRISON KEILLOR

IT'S been a noisy week here at the *New Yorker*. Last Monday morning I myself had the temerity to launch an attack on our esteemed editress, Mrs Evans, or as she prefers to be called in her working environment Miss Tina Brown (Lord alone knows why but, being English, I guess she has her own ways of doing things). Some folks do, especially those who come from England which is where she comes from, as does her husband with whom I have no quarrel. Not as yet leastways.

Well, my little letter in which I called her "a talentless bitch" certainly put the proverbial cat among the woodchucks.

Miss Brown, normally as cool and calm as a cucumber in Mrs Smorgasbord's cucumber-patch, could scarce contain her ire. No sirree. There was one lady looking like a racoon in a salt-box.

Come Tuesday morning what do I find on the front page of my daily newspaper? "Garrison needs a rabies shot — says *New Yorker* Editor."

Then I go on to read that I was once an *enfant terrible* and now I'm a hasbeen.

Well let me tell you this. Whatever Miss Brown thinks, the boys in the bar will tell you different.

Take old man Toksvig, who used to do cartoons for editor Willie Shawn when he wasn't running his feed-store. He says:

"Yup! Magazine no goddam good since that Mrs Evans done took it over. It's gone to the coyotes."

And he can say a lot more too when he chooses. But he doesn't need to.

No one buys the magazine now. Not the folks that count don't. *(Continues for 94 pages in similar vein)*

• CAROLINE QUENTIN TARANTINO •

"Do you wanna get fucking married or what?"

Steve Seita

AITKEN IN DRAMATIC NEW SHOCK

by Our Political Staff
Lunchtime O'Sleaze

THE world of Westminster was rocked to its foundations yesterday by the news that top Tory Jonathan Aitken had not been involved in any allegations of sleaze in the past 24 hours.

Aitken sensationally was not accused of:

● Selling arms to Iraq
● Selling arms to Iran
● Selling arms to Mohammed Al-Fayed for resale in the Harrods Firearms Department (3rd Floor next to Islamic jewellery and Ladies Haberdashery)

Cross Head of Nolan Committee

However Aitken last night hit back angrily at his critics. "I have no recollection of not being involved in any scandal," he said, "and even if I did I was not aware of not being involved nor of not having any recollection of not being involved. Would you please excuse me. I have a Mr Pol Pot waiting to see me about an invoice."

Mr Taki Takalotofcokeupthenos is 72.

THE GRAUNIAD
Correction

In our report on Mr Aitken's involvement with a number of distinguished Arabian businessmen an unfortunate typographical error was introduced. Thus the sentence read "Aitken tried to procure girls for the Arabs". This should of course have read "grills", a favourite snack for Middle Eastern dignitaries, and it was quite understandable for Mr Aitken to provide grills for his friends at any time day or night in the privacy of their own sauna. Big grills, little grills, Danish grills, and of course grills dressed up as French maids. We regret any confusion caused by this misprint.

"Already! My God, that IS premature"

IN THOSE days there came to pass a terrible plague of sleaze, and it filled the land like an evil cancer. And all good people were shocked and dismayed at the way monstrous creatures roamed at will, spreading the pestilence far and wide.

And all respect for the rulers was lost as the poisonous vermin and reptiles undermined the fabric of the nation.

But, lo, there rose up at last a champion to fight the sleaze dragons. St Jonathan was a rich young noble who had spent his days in the country of Arslikhan, helping the rich and ignoring the poor.

"Good people!" he cried. "Enough is enough! I will undertake to rid the nation of these hideous monsters!" So the saintly figure proclaimed, boldly reading from his autocue.

Then he set forth with his trusty writ in one hand, and a wallet full of Arab money in the other.

But sadly he was surrounded by evil hacks and forced to resign.

© The Society for the Promotion of Conservative Knowledge.

NEW CD OFFER!

GUNS AND DOLLS

STARRING JONATHAN AITKEN

HIT SONGS INCLUDE:
ALI, GET YOUR GUN (FROM ME)
SUING IN THE RAIN
PUTTING OUT THE WRITS
STAYING IN THE RITZ
SAUDI PACIFIC
I'M GOING TO WASH THAT MAN RIGHT OUT OF THE TORY PARTY
(THAT'S ENOUGH SONGS. ED)

ATTROCIOUS

TACKY

(The World's 2nd Worst Columnist)

Aitken is Wonderful

JONATHAN Aitken is head and shoulders above the dirty little lefties on the *Guardian*. I met him camel-racing in Bahrain with my old friend, Prince Ahm-Al-Ite, who was with Russian attache Konrad Kalashnikov and the American Davis Cup finalist J.D. Slazenger. Unlike the greasy little Trots on the *Guardian*, Jonathan has a beautiful wife and daughter, both of whom put inches on this little Greek boy's column (geddit?). Insiders (Jonathan Aitken) tell me that Jonathan will be the next Prime Minister. So watch out leftie scum because he'll kill you when he gets in.

Streisand Makes Me Sick

BARBRA Streisand makes me sick. She can't sing and she makes me sick. She couldn't even play tennis for Greece, like I did. I met her once in 1970 in Sniffer's Club on 78th and 94th in the Big Bagel. She was surrounded by a lot of creeps like Rad Zaldeberg, Morty Schwarzlutz, and Marion Pimms, ex-wife of perfume tycoon Milmot Pimms. *(Who are these people? Ed.)*

And you know what the non-tennis-playing Jewish Princess said to the poor little Greek boy? No?

"No thank you, Mr Taki, I do not do cocaine, but I'm sure you will find a buyer amongst your rather disgusting friends."

What a loser. No wonder she makes me sick! She never even played judo for Greece. Get a life, Barbra!

NEXT WEEK: Taki on Jonathan Aitken and Barbra Streisand.

A Taxi Driver writes

Each week a well-known cabbie is invited to comment on an issue of topical importance.

This week: **Dave Dibbs** (cab no. 724364) on the Electrocution of Nicholas Ingram

■ Those Americans guv, they're bleedin' barbarians. Blimey! Keeping a bloke waitin' for 12 years and then fryin' 'im live in an electric chair. I mean, they send 200,000 volts straight through your system and your eyes pop out, your brain boils, and it's ages before you're even dead! I don't want to even think about it! They have to shave all your arms an' that, put that gel stuff on you so the electricity goes right in you, and they put a thing on your head and the chair's right next to where you spend your final hours. It's sickenin'! I mean, it's inhuman! It's barbaric.

You know what they should do to people like Ingram? String 'im up! It's the only language he understands.

I 'ad that Pierrepoint in the back of the cab once. A real gentleman...

NEXT WEEK: Jim Le Fanu (cab no. 127118) on the implications of London's proposed hospital reorganisation.

THE MEMOIRS OF JOHN COLE

Serialised exclusively in Private Eye

------ CHAPTER ONE ------

THE THOTCHER YEARS

Hondootedly Mossis Thotcher chilliconcarne ambrosiacreamrice sunblockfactortwentyseven Sea Change In Brutush Politics panis angelicus nissan toyota Moster Edward Heath monteverdi bellisarius chiaroscuro lesterpiggott sunflower margerine Bockbenchers' Revolt pierodellafrancesca tetleybitter budleigh salterton tasmania Falklands Factor tuttifrutti bananarama shiboom shiboom Cat Among The Pigeons. Moster Francis Pym guiseppe verdi benetton pergolese stabat mater catamaran Arthur Scargill limpopo lynbarber butheleizi. Red Faces In Wostminster hondetoit andante con moto pollyputthekettleon Moster Norman Tobbit Cat Among The Pigeons Again *(continued for rest of book)*.

TOMORROW: The Cat Among The Pigeons

"It wasn't so much your policies, Jesus. You got the presentation all wrong!"

LETTERS TO THE EDITOR

From Sir Herbert Gusset

SIR—As the whole nation girds its loins to celebrate the defeat of the Boche 50 years ago, your readers may like to know of the preparations being made in one West Country village to commemorate the moment when this little island stood alone against the jackbooted ranks of European tyranny. Our aim is to recreate, for the benefit of the younger generation, the experience of "VE-Day 1945" exactly as it happened, minute-by-minute.

Our programme (provisional) is as follows:

8 a.m. Raising of Canadian flag over tower of St Ivel's church to show solidarity with the gallant fishermen of Newfoundland against the halibut-snatchers of Madrid and their friends in Brussels.

9 a.m: Village Hall. Day-long film show arranged by the good offices of Master Kevin Balon, the elder son of our local publican, to include selected home video recordings of *Inspector Morse Investigates*, *Dallas* and *Twin Peaks* (some episodes missing).

11 a.m: Parade of historic "war-time" vehicles round the sports field to include 1955 Hillman Imp; Hercules "Kestrel" drop-handled tourer bike c. 1951; milk float; as used by Webster's Dairy 1963-1971; Atco lawn-mower, the "Dorset Punch" (still in regular use by old Tom Duggan to mow churchyard and cricket square!)

12.00: St Ivel's Church. Grand VE-Day Service of Reconciliation. Speakers: Mrs Ulrike Choldmondeley-Ffoulkes (formerly Fraulein von Zeppelin) on "The Great Nation that is Germany". N.B. This event, suggested by Rev Dawlish, does not have the full support of the village VE-Day committee.

1 pm - midnight (approx.)

Lamb and Flag public house. Re-enactment by veterans of World War II of how we survived the dark days of the Blitz, 1940-1945.

A select group of veterans take refuge in the cellar of the building until the All-Clear siren is heard. Refreshments kindly provided by mine host, Mr Montague Balon. These include such familiar "austerity beverages" as Hofmeister Extra lager and a special bottle of Auld Hirohito's 100% Genuine "Scotch" Whisky brought back from Duty-Free Singapore last year by Lt. Col. Buffy Frobisher after a visit to his son Ronald in Brisbane, Australia.

12 midnight - 8 a.m (approx.): Special VE-Day "Commemorative Silence", to be observed by all those present, broken only by peaceful snores.

This will serve as a fitting climax to a truly unforgettable day.

I remain, sir, your obedient servant,

H. GUSSET
The Anderson Shelter,
Bernard St. Manning, Dorset.

ADVERTISEMENT

Grand VE Warehouse Sale

To honour those who laid down their lives in World War II, British Gnome Stores are proud to offer the following items at VEry affordable prices

MESSERSCHMITT

MESSERSCHMITT 109 WASHING MACHINE AND TUMBLE-DRYER
WAS £186.99
NOW £185.99

THE "BUSHIDO CAMIKAZICORDER with 250mm Zoom Lens and Self-Edit
WAS £499.99
NOW £599.99

1 CASE SPARKLING VICHY WATER
WAS £24.60
NOW 60 Deutschmarks

FREE with each item 1 Winston Churchill Freedom Mug hand-crafted in the Republic of China.

THE KLAUS BARBICUE
Perfect for long summer evenings. With 1 bag easy-to-light "Charkohl"
WAS £13.50
NOW £13.50

BRITISH GNOME STORES (UK) IS A SUBSIDIARY OF THE NISSAN CORPORATION, FRANKFURT

Core Curriculum Examination

Option 94: **THE SECOND WORLD WAR 1939-1945**

MULTIPLE CHOICE

1. What was the Second World War called?

a) The First World War
b) The Second World War
c) The Wars of the Roses

2. What were the dates of the 1939-45 war?

a) Take That
b) Eric Cantona
c) 1939-45

3. Who won the war?

a) McDonalds
b) Arnold Schwarzenegger
c) The women of Britain

4. Who were the opposing teams in the final?

a) West Germany vs Brazil
b) Stephen Hendry vs Jimmy White?
c) Zardac vs Monglog (© Sega Games 1994)

5. Who was Prime Minister during the war? (There are no marks for this question)

a) Adolf Hitler
b) Winston Silcott
c) Germaine Greer

Take as long as you like and don't finish if you can't be bothered.

Issued to all schools by the Dept of Education

A GNOME SPECIAL VE-CD OFFER

THE SONGS THAT WON THE WAR!

Thrill again to such Wartime Wonders as

● **Ronnie Essoldo and His Essoldians:** *"Put Another Sausage In The Oven, Mother"* (vocalist 'Rambling' Al Coren)

● **Dame Rita Cadillac:** *"There's An Apple Tree In My Heart"*

● **Ted Millie and Billy Watford:** *"Bend Over, Adolf, And We'll Kick You Up Your Axis"*

● **Dame Gertie Mitford:** *"Keep The Spam Fritters Burning"*

● **The Christopher Silvester Strings:** *"Londoner's Diary"*

● **The Band of the 78th/33rd Queen's Own Squadron:** *"The Bomber Harris March"*

● **Comic Monologue.** Sidney "Put That Light Out!" Tosh: *"The Day I Lost My Crumpet"*

● **Stanley Gibbons and The Gibbonaires:** *"The Winston Waltz"* (original Savoy Hotel recording with authentic air raid)

Plus hundreds of others that you're glad you've forgotten.

Hurry, hurry, before interest wanes!

Peter McLie

The World's Worst Columnist

AM I the only one to have noticed that it is almost 50 years since the end of the Second World War?

Should we not mark this historic occasion in some way?

Perhaps the Queen Mother could repeat her performance by coming out on the balcony of Buckingham Palace?

And surely Dame Vera Lynn is still alive somewhere, and could be invited out of retirement to regale us with some of her much-loved wartime hits, such as *Congratulations* and *Puppet On A String*?

On second thoughts, maybe not. Perhaps it is just as well that we ignored the whole thing completely.

After all, folk are not interested in that old stuff any more.

MY FRIEND Andrew Wilson has bought a new pair of pyjamas with a button on the trousers instead of the old cord.

I find the world is divided into two groups — those who like buttons and those who prefer cords. And those whose pyjamas are fastened with a wee zip. (*That's three. Ed.*)

Are you a "cordie" or a "zippie"? Do write in and tell me and then I can fill up my column with another paragraph next time.

WHO *says the British can't make sitcoms any more?*

I have been watching a new series on the BBC called Dad's Army.

It is set in the Second World War and is absolutely hilarious.

Every line was a winner. Every situation was a hoot.

Mrs McLie and myself roared with laughter.

They should put it on every night, instead of all that dreadful rubbish imported from America, like Heartbreak High and Steptoe and Son.

ONE *of the perils of getting pissed every lunchtime (shurely 'getting older'? Ed) is that you begin to forget your own name. I have asked my friend Andrew Wilson if he has any idea who I am, but he has forgotten his own name as well.*

If you have the remotest clue who I am, please write in and tell me. Just send a postcard to Peter McWho, The World's Worst Trouserpress, Somewhere in London.

"What I find really astonishing is the fact that nobody's used the word 'resonance' tonight"

That Soviet VE Day Peace Parade In Full

Red Square, Thursday

On Podium
(underneath special Peace Logo showing Hammer, Sickle and French Fries, kindly sponsored by McDonald's)

President Yeltsin and Bottle
(shurely 'Mrs Yeltsin'? Ed)

President Clintstone and Saxophone
(shurely 'Hillary Roddam Testosterone III'? Ed)

Herr Reichskanzler Adolf Kohl and Mrs Braun

Unidentified Man in Suit (possibly J. Major)

The Procession Was Formed As Follows

3 Regiments of the Elite Internal Warfare Special Troops, fresh from their triumph in Chechnya

2,000 T-74 Anti-Personnel Carriers (originally 4,000, but the other half were sold to the Chechens by their drivers for a bottle of vodka)

10,000 veterans from the Great Patriotic War over Afghanistan hobbling past on one leg

A fly-past of 20,000 Ilyshin Aeroflot bombers, most of which crash on suburbs of Moscow due to engine failure

50,000 veterans of Stalin's Gulags, celebrating the Great Patriotic Purges of 1941-1980

The ex-KGB Regiment (now renamed "Group Fourski" and "Securicorski") marching past in ill-fitting uniforms

The Mafia Guard, who fire ceremonial 3,000-round salute at each other

10-mile queue for bread follows procession

Floats Representing Soviet Entertainment During The Great Patriotic War

1st Float: Vera Lynnski singing selection of much-loved wartime hits, including "We'll Never Meet Again" and "We're Going To Throw You Over The White Cliffs Of Dover"

2nd Float: Cliff Richardov singing "We're All Going On A Siberian Holiday".

3rd Float: The Glenn Millerski Orchestra playing "The Chechnyugoo Choo-Choo".

The crowd then joined in a patriotic chorus of "Down with Yeltsin".

Tonight on Soviet TV

"What Did You Do In The War, Big Brother?" How Soviet radio helped to win the war by establishing a reputation for fearless lying.

Those German VE Day Celebrations In Full

Victory Over England Day

Herr Reichsführer Kohl today took the salute in Berlin as thousands of goosestepping bankers celebrated the fall of the pound and the glorious triumph of the EU (Germany) over the last pockets of British resistance. *(That's enough celebrations. Ed.)*

"Alright — I'll do another bloody mammoth"

HE KEPT US LAUGHING THROUGH THE DARK DAYS

ONE man more than any other kept the nation smiling through the long years that led up to 8 May 1995.

"Cheeky Chappie" Chris Evans broadcast round the clock with his own optimistic brand of irrepressible humour.

With catch-phrases like: "Toot if you've got a big one", "Don't ring me now, missus, I'm on the toilet" and "I want another £1 million, Mr Birt, or I'll go back to the telly", Evans caught the mood of the nation.

Who could forget his brilliant, heart-warming, morale-boosting catch-phrases, such as "Toot if you've got a big one" *(Haven't we had this one before? Ed)*.

SHE WAS THE NATION'S PIN-UP

NO ONE did more for the nation's morale in the dark days of 1995 than the celebrated comic-strip heroine Liz, whose adventures appeared every day on the front page of the *Daily Telegraph*.

As one veteran World War II historian, General Sir Max Hastings, remembers: "She kept all our peckers up. In every episode her dress revealed a little more. And the whole nation was agog to see if she would ever strip off altogether."

General Hastings is 94.

ADVERTISEMENT

TO COMMEMORATE Victory in Europe, the Royal Mail is issuing a special set of stamps to commemorate the work of the United Nations.
There will be five special stamps showing:

- UN forces withdrawing from Croatia
- UN forces withdrawing from Bosnia
- UN forces withdrawing from Rwanda
- UN forces not entering Chechnya
- Boutros Boutros-Ghali enjoying a large lunch

The UN stamps are guaranteed not to stick on either side and to curl up and fall off the envelope.

Price: £2,999 for set of five

YOUR CHANCE TO JOIN IN THE 1995 COMPLETE FAILURE IN EUROPE CELEBRATIONS!

Poetry Corner

**In Memoriam:
U Nu, former Prime Minister of Burma**

So. Farewell then
U Nu.

Who were you?
No one knows.

But
U Nu!

Geddit?

E.J. Thribb (17½)

"It's the new UN deterrent"

Lines To Commemorate The Historic Decision By The Controller Of BBC2 To Discontinue *The Late Show*

'Twas in the year nineteen hundred and ninety five,
That Mr Michael Jackson decided the Late Show could
                              no longer survive,
He was the Controller of BBC2,
And he decided that this unexpected move was the only
                              thing he could do.

No more in the title sequence would the wolf howl at the
                              moon —
A sign for the majority of viewers that they would be
                              going to sleep soon,
When they heard what was to be the cultural bill of fayre,
All across the nation they would at once to their
                              beds repair.

Typical of such a night's viewing would be
A discussion of a new Korean Expressionist movie,
Or perhaps a naked dance troupe from the USA,
Or maybe from the Royal Court Upstairs a
                              controversial new play.

Music lovers too would always get their fill
Of the Country and Western singers frae bonny
                              Nashville.

Typical of their southern rural art,
Would be a 20-minute version of "Your Cheatin' Heart".

For those who are to the visual arts inclined,
There would be reviews of De Kooning and Yves Klein,
And for those who like a good book on their shelf,
There would be lengthy profiles of serious authors
                              like Will Self.

And most of all surely as this landmark passes,
We will remember the presenter with the
                              extraordinary glasses,
Sarah Dunant was this seminal figure
(Who evoked from the philistines at *Private Eye*
                              the occasional snigger).

But who can forget her animated diction
Or her grasp of contemporary Portuguese fiction?
She was but the first of many a bright star,
And one thinks immediately of young Waldermar
(His surname I'm afraid I cannot recall.
At 11.20 at night one is far from on the ball).

Then there was a Scottish lass tall and proud,
And her name I think was Kirsty McLeod,
Or was it possibly not that but Tracy Wark?
I'm not sure, but she was not the bearded fellow
                              called Mark.

He regularly appeared with an Irishman
                              called Tom Paulin,
Who no doubt contributed to the fact that the figures
                              were falling.
But so it was until the fateful day,
When the hard-pressed Controller had his final say.

"We may consider it the flagship of BBC Arts,
But research shows that the viewers think it's a bunch
                              of pretentious farts."

©*William Rees-McGonagall*

GIANT LOTTERY FRAUD
Knacker fails to swoop

by Our Heritage Staff
Ben Pimlottery

THOUSANDS of police failed to swoop today on the Tory MP at the centre of a complex £12 million National Lottery scam.

The man, who cannot be named, is Winston Churchill, who has pocketed £12 million which would otherwise have gone to charities.

The ingenious scheme involved the senior members of the Churchill family putting it about that an unnamed American foundation was prepared to pay them millions of dollars for the late Sir Winston Churchill's priceless collection of laundry bills and bus tickets.

You Scratch My Card...

Mr Churchill then thought of a series of "winning numbers" — in this case 12 33 30 00 — then wrote them down and passed them to a friend (Stephen Dorrell).

The friend then paid out immediately, leaving Mr Churchill the biggest single winner since the lottery was launched last November.

I'll Scratch Yours

Experts were saying last night that there is only a one in 14 million chance of being Winston Churchill's grandson.

"I am delighted with this win," said Mr Churchill. "The money will not spoil me. I am a greedy, self-satisfied Tory already."

Asked whether it would not have been simpler just to give the Churchill archive to the nation, Mr Churchill said: "The problem with that would be that I would not make a huge amount of money for doing nothing. But this way, £12 million that might otherwise have been wasted on Oxfam, Save the Children, leukaemia research or other whingeing charities, has all been diverted to me and will provide much-needed alimony for many years to come."

Mr Churchill concluded: "Yes, it will change my wife."

Poetry Corner

In Memoriam: Lines On The Death Of Ginger Rogers, Aged 83

So. Farewell then
Ginger Rogers.

Famous partner of Fred
Astaire, who is also
Dead.

Tap-tap-tappity-tap.
Tap.
That is how we will
Remember you.

Tappity-tappity-tap-tap-tap
Tap-tap.
And so on.

E.J. Thribb (17½)

Radio Highlights

That New Youth-Appeal Archers In Full

(Signature tune. Rap version of traditional Dum-Di-Dum-Di-Dum-Di-Dum by Snoop Doggy Labrador)

Kate Aldridge: OK Mum, so I've had a joint. A spliff. Shit. Smack. Grass. Weed. Hash. Speed. Pot. Mariellafrostrup! What the hell do you care? You're just so square, why don't you just chill out, get in the groove and give me some more space, OK?

Mrs Aldridge: I don't know what your father will have to say.

Kate: That old Daddy-O! He can get out of my face! He doesn't even know I'm having an abortion and I'm joining an order of Lesbian Druid Motorway Protestors!

Roy: Hi Kate! Hi Mrs Archer! I just came round to borrow a cup of heroin. I've just been down the Bull meeting my crack dealer but he's been machinegunned in cold blood by the Ambridge Triads!

Kate: Wow! Happening! Gear! Fab! Simon Mayo!

(Continued on 94KHz)

"It was a messy divorce"

US FURY AT MAJOR'S INVITATION

by Our Outrage Staff
Lunchtime O'Klahoma

THERE WAS widespread indignation in the United States yesterday at Downing Street's announcement that the Prime Minister was to play host to the President of the Oklahoma and Michigan Far Right Anti-Federalist Militia, Mr Adam McGerard.

Downing Street defended the decision, saying that Mr McGerard and his colleagues, though guilty of mass murder, had a democratic mandate in the United States (0.0003% in the latest opinion poll).

"It is time," said a spokesman, "for dialogue and understanding rather than casting blame on people for terrorist outrages."

He continued: "The militias have a very real role to play in the future of Michigan and Oklahoma and it is only sensible for them to be included in negotiations, not to mention photo opportunities with the Prime Minister."

Oklahome Rule

US suggestions that Major was just trying to suck up to the extreme Right at home were discounted.

"It's not realistic," said the PM's office, "to expect the militias to decommission their weapons without some gesture of good faith by the American government.

Gun Ho

"President Clinton should issue a general amnesty for all militiamen and release the prisoners from jail at once."

"Was it something I said?"

Poetry Corner

**In Memoriam
Harold Wislon**

So. Farewell then
Harold Wilson.

Prime minister and
Statesman.

With your pipe
And Gannex macintosh
You were a
Much-loved figure,

Very similar to Mike Yarwood.

"The pound in your
Pocket."
That was your catchphrase.

"The white heat of
Technology."
That was another.

"A week is a long time
In politics."
That was the other one.

But Keith's mum said
You were a shifty
Little chap.

She couldn't understand
How that nice Mary
Could put up with you.

E.J. Thribblon of Drivelaux (79¾)

Yes, it's the girl the Grauniad tried to gag!

GLENDA GREER JOINS THE EYE!!

THAT Suzanne Moore. Aren't-chasickofher??

With her bird's nest shoes and her fuck-me hair and her bloody great boobs hanging out all over the place, like a couple of koalas hanging off a eucey tree!?!!

I say this fat old slag doesn't know the difference between history and hysterectomy??!??

Let's have less of Suzanne, not more. Geddit? (Just Germaine's little joke!?)

THAT Alan Rusbridger. What a wanker!?!

With his bird's nest glasses and fuck-me sports jacket, he wouldn't put my piece attacking Suzanne Moore into the Guardian??! He's the editor, stoopid!? I reckon he's got as much brains as a kookaburra on Prozac!!!

WHY are the younger generation so rude? They have no manners and no respect!?

That Suzanne Moore, for example, with her bird's nest column and her fuck-me feminism?!?!

She's an even bigger tosser than little Rubbisher?!

And that's saying something!?

Doesn't she realize that I am the gal who put the Women's Movement on the map. When she was just a flabby little baby in her bird's nest nappies, sucking her fuck-me dummy?!?

Fuck me!!!?

© *World copyright Dr Germaine Greer, Reader in English Literature, University of Cambridge.*

WISLON
The Tributes Flow In

Edward Heath

WHEN I was Prime Minister, it has to be said that I did a much better job of it than he did. I particularly remember the way he let me down when I was leading Britain into the European Union, one of my great triumphs, of which there were many. People often said that I was the greatest prime minister of this country and they were right. In addition I am a world class yachtsman, a fine organist and have also written some excellent books about myself.

Woy Jenkins

HAROLD was a most agweeable colleague, who enjoyed fine wines, good food and civilised conversation. We wegularly lunched together when he was Pwime Minister. Perhaps his gweatest stwoke of genius was to appoint me Chancellor, in which gweat office of state, it has to be said, I was a twiumphant success.

Paul McCartney

THE Sixties were a great time for us. We had a load of hits and that. And we met Harold Wilson, I think. He was a lovely bloke and he knew all our songs and he gave us an OBE because we were the greatest band of all time. Do you want one of my wife's vegetableburgers?

Denis Healey

I WAS the first to know that Harold was going to resign, when he told the Cabinet that he had had enough. That was two years before anyone else knew, which I think shows how influential I was.

John Major

HAROLD Wilson was a brilliant prime minister, though at the time few people realised it. With his grey hair and glasses, his love of cricket and his vision of a classless society, he was much derided, and he had terrible trouble with the divisions in his party over Europe. Yet history will come to recognise him as the longest-serving minister since Margaret Thatcher.

Tony Blair

HAROLD will always be remembered for the way he modernised the Labour party and led it to victory after more than a decade of Tory domination. In my view he was a genius.

Margaret Thatcher

I ALWAYS had the greatest possible respect for myself.

Mike Yarwood

YOU know... (Contd pp 94-180)

"I understand Lord Goodman has come on ahead to fix it up…"

'ABSOLUTELY USELOUS' TO END

by Our TV Staff
Marcus Bartsman

THE long-running farce "Absolutely Uselous" is set to close this week after a hilarious final episode in which the outrageous blonde star (played by Virginia Bumley) is humiliated in the House of Commons.

Virginia, who has won no awards and no critical acclaim for her role as the tough-talking bitch who wants to close down the NHS, has become one of the country's least-loved comic figures and no one will mourn her passing.

"All bad things have to come to an end and even a really terrible show like this cannot go on indefinitely," said producer John Major.

"The problem is" he continued, "that we have no more ideas. What could Virginia do that is more stupid and more unpleasant that what she has already done? No, she's going to quit while she is behind."

So, have we seen the last of the fag-and-drink hating harpie? We do hope so.

Virginia Bottomley looks 78.

PLOTS! I'M SURROUNDED BY PLOTS!

SIR HAROLD WILSON RIP

JOHN BYRNE

SLIPFLOITERS

IN CANNES

🙂 It's that French Connection again! Perhaps it's in Mr **Hackman**'s **Genes**!?! Is he just **Scacchi-ng Greta**'s back? Or is he up to White Mischief?

🙂 **Van Damme** it! Some guys have all the luck! Claude's got **Demi Moore** than his fair share of the beautiful girls! It's a **Cin-dy** that he's got Miss **Crawford** as well! There's nothing like a Damme for the Belgian Beefcake!?

🙂 Not so much Reservoir Dogs as Marina Mutts!! That's the message for tough guy actor **Nick Nolte** and new "Pet" **Petula Clark**! I'm sure they're going to be going "Downtown" in Cannes tonight!

🙂 Isn't life a beach?! It is for Britain's **Emma Thompson**, the Shakespearean star caught here for once without hubby **Ken**!! 2 piece or not 2 piece, that is the swimsuit question!

🙂 A slimline **Arnold Schwarzenegger** flies in with the **Isabella** of the Ball! Miss **Rossellini** of course! Will this affair Terminate here? Or is it all True Lies what they are saying down Cannes way? Hasta la vista – maybe?! *(You're fired – Hasta la vista to you. Ed)*

(That's enough pisspoor captions to dreary film PR photos written by sad hacks who aren't in Cannes)

HOUSE OF COMMONS
OFFICIAL REPORT

PARLIAMENTARY DEBATES

HANZ-Z-Z-ARD

2.32 Emergency Debate on the Threat Posed By Lord Nolan to the Snouts-In-Trough Industry.

Sir Bufton Tufton (Lymeswold, Con.): Mrs Speaker, I am sure you would agree that it is a tremendous tribute to the honour of this House that so many of us — indeed all of us — have taken the afternoon off from our very important consultancies to appear in the Commons.

(Cries of "here, here")

We face what is undoubtedly the greatest threat in the past 800 years to everything which parliament stands for. I refer of course to that right of every Member of this House (especially on our side) to use our positions to make as much money on the side as is humanly possible. This fellow Nolan is attempting to destroy the liberties which we take every week.

(Members wave bank statements amid cries of "String Nolan up!")

Mr Slithy Tove (Sleazewold, Con.): May I ask a simple question, for which incidentally I am only being paid £6000. In view of the outrageous suggestion by Lord Nolan that honourable members are in some way being paid to ask questions, could I ask who was the stupid idiot who first asked Lord Nolan to stick his nose in our trough?

Rt. Hon. John Major (the Prime Minister): In answer to my honourable friend, it was me. When I appointed Lord Nolan it was done with the very highest of motives — i.e. to push sleaze under the carpet until everyone had forgotten about it. What I forgot was that eventually he would produce a report. Therefore I now propose that we should push the report under the carpet instead.

(Huge cheers of relief from Tories and cries of men on mobile phones shouting "It's ok, darling, you can keep the range rover. See you at ten" and "It's OK, sweetybum, you can keep the flat. See you at six")

Grocer Heath (Blubber-on-the-Take, Con.) I've been a member of this House for 60 years, and I can assure Lord Nolan, whoever he is, that I have never seen or heard of any member acting dishonourably in any way. I myself, on a basic salary of £40,000, have managed to afford a house in Salisbury worth several million pounds, not to mention my various yachts, my priceless paintings and other works of art. How dare anyone ask me how I got all this money? It is an outrageous intrusion on the privacy of an outstanding former Prime Minister, of impeachable integrity.

(Cheers of "Good old Grocer – first thing you've ever said that makes sense")

Madam Speaker: I call Sir Jerry Wiggin.

Sir Jerry Wiggin (Great Crook, Con.): Madam Speaker, you have asked me to apologise to the House for being caught out. I unreservedly and humbly would like to suggest that I have done nothing wrong. And certainly not anything which the rest of you aren't just as guilty of. OK, so I used someone else's name on a order paper. But what I would ask the House, in all lack of humility, is which of them could put their hands on their wallets and honestly say that they wouldn't have done the same, if it was a matter of covering up their entirely legitimate backhanders from various industries?

(There are sobs from the backbenches as Tory MPs are moved to tears at the thought of having to give up their consultancies)

Wiggin: Would anyone care for a South African orange? I have several crates outside in the car park, thanks to my highly important fact-finding mission to that country on behalf of the Citrus Growers Association of Weston-super-Mare.

Madam Speaker: It's OK, Jerry, we've already forgotten all about it. The important thing is that we have, by the high quality of this debate, upheld the honour of this House.

(Huge cheers as MPs rush to celebrate their victory over Nolan by taking their "researchers" off for agreeable dinners in SW3)

That Vote In Full

For Snouts-In-Trough industry *360*
Against Nolan . . . . *everyone else*

OPERA CHOICE

LEONARDO IN EXTREMIS

by Giovanni Rumpoli

THIS little-known opera, unperformed until now, tells the delightful story of an eccentric merchant, Don Leonardi Ingrami, and his wife Rosalinda who decide to set up an opera festival in the peaceful village of Garsingtoni.

It is a great success as rich folk come from far and near with their bottles of champagne and hampers full of Coronation chicken.

They all sing the great chorus — "Viva Fortnumi e Masoni".

Then trouble starts when angry villagers go to the Environmental Health Inspectori and demand that the opera should be stopped. They sing the chorus "Nessun Dorma" ("No one can sleep").

Poor Don Leonardi is brought before a Judge and loses the case, singing the famous aria "Tuto Perduto" ("I've lost all my money").

Fate however intervenes when the Judge has a change of heart and the villagers are sent packing. Donna Rosalinda sings the final aria "Bastardi Rusticani".

© *Alexander Waugh in conjunction with Classic FM.*

PRIVATISED INDUSTRY CHAIRMAN'S SALARY RISE SHAKER

The Alternative Rocky Horror Service Book

No. 94: The Sacrament of Holy Non-Matrimony

The President: Is everyone all right?

All: Yes, thanks, Kevin (or it may be Simon, according to the name of the ordinand).

President: Great. Well let's kick off with a piece of music.

A CD shall then be played, belonging to either the non-bride or the non-groom, signifying the coming together of their two record collections. It may be An Whiter Shade Of Pale by Procul Harum, or An Bridge Over Troubled Water by Simon and Garfunkel.

President: We are gathered here together to join these two, N and M (here he shall name the prospective partners) in the state of holy cohabitation, which is a state ordained by the Church of England Working Committee On Alternative Modes Of Relationship And Family Structure in order to show that the Church is caring, compassionate, non-judgemental and really attuned to the needs of a changing society.

All: Get on with it.

THE VOWS

President: Do you (here he turns to the man) take this woman (or he may say 'man') as your lawful wedded partner, to have it away with, for as long as ye both shall feel like it?

Both: We do.

President: If anyone knows of any reason why these two should not move into one or other of their two places and rent the other one out in case it doesn't work out, ye are to declare it.

Archbishop: It doesn't seem quite right to me.

All: Shut up.

President: OK, let's sing.

HYMN

"I'm Not Getting Married In The Morning", from 100 Secular Hymns For Today.

ADDRESS

President: Our Lord Himself never married and nor did his mother. I think this shows that "living in sin", as it used to be laughingly called, is a positive moral choice, which in a very real sense shows genuine commitment. Whereas marriage is merely giving in to social pressure in the most feeble-minded and bourgeois way.

All: Ooh-ah-Cantuar.

The couple will then give each other a ring on their mobiles to signify their state of temporary togetherness.

THE DISMISSAL

President: Well, that's about it then. That was all pretty pointless, wasn't it?

The congregation will then proceed to the nearest pub (or it may be the Pizza Hut) to the strains of Mendelssohn's Partnership March (or it may be Alan Clark's The Crumpet Voluntary).

© Carey and Sharey Productions 1995

NEW IN THE EYE!

JULIE BULLSHIT

MEN — aren'tchasickof-them? I am. I really am. Men. Sick. Of. Them. I. Am.

WOMEN — don'tcha-luv'em? I do. They're great. I. Love. Them. No — it's men I'm sick of!!

MEN — aren'tchasick-ofthem? I love women. Yes, I do but I'm sick of men!!!

P.S. Men and Women? I'm sick of one and I love the other! Guess which?! Clue: It isn't women I'm sick of because I love them. It's men because they make me sick.

© Julie Bulldyke.

Reprinted from the Sunday Times News Review.

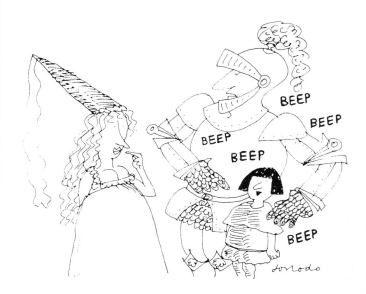

"Sorry — it my pager"

GLENDA SLAGG

The Girl With the Sack-Me Shoes!!?!

● SO THE Powergen bosses have given themselves a fortune?!! So what?!
Wouldn't you if you were in their shoes?! You bet you would!?! So shut up Mr Green-Eyed General Public!!?! Just because you haven't won the Lottery!?!?

■ NICHOLAS Scott!? What a fuss about nothing!?! Just because he ran over a toddler after he'd had a few?! Who hasn't?!! There's no reason to drive him out of office?!!?

☐ NICHOLAS Scott!! What a swine!? Resign at once! That's Glenda's advice to this Pig of the Year!? You nearly murdered a cute little French baby in your debauched post-party fumblin' with your secretary!?!
You can't walk away from this one Nicky-Boy!?! Do the decent thing and string yourself up!?!

○ HERE they are — Glenda's Midsummer Machos!?!

The Bishop of Bath and Wells — come and not live in sin with me Big Jim!! And bring your mitre!?

Julie Burchill — now she's a bloke I really fancy her!?! Mmmmmm!??!

Matthew Amroliwala — Mr BBC Bradford!! Crazy name, crazy guy.

Byeeeeeeee!?

Poetry Corner

In Memoriam
The Modern Review

So. Farewell
Then
*The Modern
Review* magazine.

You are no
Longer
Coming out.

Unlike your
Proprietor
Julie Burchill.

Now no one
Will be able
To read you.

Just like
Before.

(E.J. Thribbchill, 17½ stone)

TV HIGHLIGHTS

The Last Days of Major

Surrender!

I only got 5 seats

Three-hour documentary charting the extraordinary final hours of the hated John Major who clings on to power in his Downing Street bunker whilst the Not Very Red Army approaches (led by Colonel Blairia). Major however refuses to accept that it is all over and still dreams of recovering the ground he has lost.

He orders in hordes of Young Conservatives and plans a new Cones offensive on the M25.
But it is too late and Major is eventually forced to commit suicide by privatising the railways.
(Only available to viewers in Scotland)

73

THOSE THATCHER MEMOIRS
— IN FULL —

Chapter 1:
THE EARLY YEARS

Forget about the early years. Let's get on to that bastard Major.

Chapters 2-94:
THAT BASTARD MAJOR

In my last book I may have mentioned the horrifying way in which, after 11 glorious years of the finest government this country has ever seen, I was viciously and cruelly betrayed by a gang of spineless wimps and Judases.

Yet the story did not end there. It has got worse. All that I worked for has been squandered and cast away by that dreadful little man with grey hair and glasses who once had the nerve to allow me to make him prime minister.

© *Murdochtrash Productions 1995*

Peter McLie

The World's Worst Columnist

WHY are all the papers devoting so much space to the silly feud between someone called Julie Burchill and a Mr Toby Young?

Outside the sleazy environs of the Groucho Club, I doubt if anyone has even heard of these scribblers.

Yet acres of newsprint are devoted to their squalid little row.

There is surely something very rotten in the state of journalism, when we are expected to take an interest in such trivial media gossip.

I AM fascinated by the row between Julie Burchill and Toby Young.

Their story has all the makings of one of the great literary feuds of all time.

Yet none of the newspapers seem to be interested.

Why are they so blind? In my view it would make a terrific film, starring Vanessa Redgrave as Mr Young and Robert Redford as Miss Burchill.

I even have a title for this epic — *The Trouser Press.*

IF I read another word about this unedifying squabble between two of London's literary nonentities, Miss Julie Burchill and Mr Toby Young, I shall be sick.

Surely there are more important issues for us columnists to devote time and space to — such as the closure of the magazine The Modern Review?

Portrait Of Dorian Not Grey

Publishing Sensation!

by Oscar Wilde-Staring-Eyes

AN EXTRAORDINARY new book has been published today which reveals the amazing secret behind the public life of former Prime Minister Mrs Dorian Blue.

The story tells of a portrait of the young Prime Minister which she keeps hanging on her wall. As the years go by, the portrait mysteriously remains unchanged whilst the Prime Minister gets progressively older and madder, with her wicked life etched irrevocably into the lines of her face.

In the end, as her teeth decay and her eyes become like hard-boiled eggs *(That's enough of this. Ed.)*

"Is there an OAP discount?"

BRILLIANT WILLS TAKES THE CAKE!

by Our Education Staff
Polly Technic (now Brooks University of Oxford)

THE HEIR to the throne has come top of the entrance exam to the exclusive, prestigious £24,000-a-day top public school St Cake's (former pupils include Stephen Fry and Radio 4's Nick Ross).

Yesterday it was announced that Prince William had beaten all-comers in what is widely accepted as the toughest academic test anywhere in the world.

Cakes Eaten

Mr Rudyard Chenevix-Kipling, the headmaster of St Cake's *(motto: Who pays, gets in)* said "There is no question of favouritism towards this particular boy. We treated him just as we would any other heir to the throne."

This is the key paper which all this year's candidates had to take:

ST CAKES ENTRANCE EXAMINATION

General Paper

1. Examine the causes of the Serbo-Croat War of 1878, with special reference to the part played by the Grand Duke of Waldegravia.

2. Clark's Theorem suggests that all solids conform to six basic laws. Name two of them and draw diagrams to illustrate their effects.

3. Solve the following equation:

$$\frac{x^3 (b+y)^3 + \sqrt{412}\ \pi}{\frac{dy}{dx} - (72^o \cos 4 \ \infty^{\pi})}$$

4. Draw a map of Australia, including the major river systems, mountain ranges, climate micro-regions and the population centres of Wanga Donga, New Neasden and Barking Greer.

5. Is your name Prince William?

Time allowed: 3 hours

Candidates need answer only 1 question.

"Quango chutney, sir?"

RGJ

GOVERNMENT HEALTH WARNING

OFFICIAL SMUG ALERT

The whole of the country is now in danger of being enveloped by smug. The recent Labour victory in the local elections has unleashed a huge cloud of hot air which has created the perfect conditions for smug. If you feel nauseous, irritable, or have difficulty taking in blair then you must turn off the television and radio, throw away the newspapers and stay in your room for the next five years.

Neil Hamilton MP cleared of sleaze allegations

There are no charges…

… and I go totally free.

It's just like the Ritz in Paris!

LETTERS TO THE EDITOR

1 Pennington Street, London E1 9XN Telephone 0171-782 5000

That Scott Report

From Lord Howe

Sir, It is quite monstrous that a mere High Court judge should seek to make pronouncements on matters about which he knows nothing. Every sentence of Lord Justice Scott's alleged report shows how ill-advised it was to appoint an outsider to give judgment on the workings of Whitehall. How could such a man possibly understand the delicate workings of government which occasionally necessitate the witholding of certain information from parliament and the public in order to protect the jobs of millions of innocent civil servants, not to mention government ministers such as myself?

Yours faithfully,
LORD HOWEDARETHEY-
ACCUSEME OF LYING,
House of Lords.

From Mr William Waldegrave

Sir, It is little short of disgraceful that the BBC should give publicity to what is only a very tentative and interim draft report by Lord Justice Scott. The learned judge was only putting forward an entirely personal view, when he wrote "having considered all the evidence and devoted five years to studying all the available documentation, there is no doubt in my mind at all that Mr Waldegrave is a barefaced liar who should resign at once".

Lord Justice Scott quite rightly submitted this provisional conclusion to the people who really knew the truth of this business, to give them the opportunity to set the record straight and wriggle out of it. It is perfectly possible that, when the final corrected report is published, it will read as follows: "In our considered view, Mr Waldegrave acted throughout as a man of unimpeachable honour as befits an Old Etonian with an agreeable wife."

Yours faithfully,
W. WALDEGRAVE,
Organo St Phosphorus,
Somerset.

From Lord Howe

Sir, It is little short of despicably monstrous that Lord Justice Scott, as a mere lawyer, should be permitted to cross-examine a senior minister of the crown such as myself. What is more, those of us who were summoned to his Star Chamber were not even allowed to be represented by lawyers who could be relied upon to lie on our behalf. We were therefore put in the very unfortunate position of having to tell our own lies, as we do in the House of Commons. Furthermore, it is nothing short of a national scandal that Lord Scott should thus have denied lucrative employment to a large number of lawyers simply in order to save the taxpayers money.

Yours faithfully,
LORD HOWEDARETHEY-
ACCUSEME OF BEING BONKERS.
House of Lords.

From Mr Simon Jenkins

Sir, As a former editor of the *Times*, I regard it as nothing short of monstrously and despicably outrageous that my friend Mr William Waldegrave should be criticised in the Scott report. No more decent, honourable and hard-working a public figure has ever been my friend. What do my colleagues in the media think they are doing attacking members of the government? It would never have happened in my time.

Yours faithfully,
SIMON JENKINS,
Grand Millennium Committee.

From Sir Geoffrey Bufton-Smith

Sir, I am in a state of incandescent rage about something or other. What it is I cannot at this moment recall. Is it this chap Nolan? Or that train in Scotland that they want to close down? No, I remember now. It is this bounder Scott. Who does he think he is, suddenly coming out with a report accusing a Conservative government of lying? Obviously he is one of these BBC lefties such as John Humphrys and Marmaduke Hussey.

Yours faithfully,
SIR GEOFFREY BUFTON-SMITH,
House of Commons.

From Lord Howe

Sir, Since my last letter I have just thought of another brilliant excuse to let the government off the hook over the so-called "Arms to Iraq" scandal. At the time in question, whenever it was, the Foreign Office received a top secret intelligence report which revealed that the Iraqi Government had acquired from South Africa a herd of highly-trained killer "Super-Gnus" which they were planning to unleash in Trafalgar Square. The only way to stop them was to give Saddam Hussein a large supply of more conventional weapons, which would persuade him into a more peaceful stance. Such subtle matters of statecraft are clearly beyond the comprehension of some jumped-up jack-in-office like Scott, which is why we said nothing about it when he questioned us in the course of his kangaroo inquisition.

Yours faithfully,
LORD HOWEDARETHEY-
ACCUSE ANYONE OF ANYTHING,
Barking.

From Mr Alan Clark

Sir, The suggestion by Justice Scott that I was in some way telling the truth during the hearings into my policy of selling arms to Iraq is quite outrageous. I resent any suggestion that I am some sort of creepy little goody-goody who goes round sneaking on the other chaps is jolly unfair. If the judge isn't careful, I'll sleep with his wife and daughters.

Yours faithfully,
ALAN CLARK,
Legover Castle, Kent.

From Sir Nicholas Lyar

Sir, I fail to understand how Lord Justice Scott appears to have let me off the hook, since I am as guilty as the next man (M. Heseltine), if not more so.

Yours faithfully,
SIR NICHOLAS LYAR,
Attorney-General,
House of Commons.

"I hear there's been a bit of a split in the Residents' Association"

SCOTT REPORT LATEST

I'm rushing it out as fast as I can

QUENTIN TORYTINO

COUNCIL OFFICES

P.45

CON

WHY DON'T YOU JUST FUCK OFF, YOU FUCKING FUCK ?!

JOHN BYRNE

BRAIN TEASER No. 94

The Cretan Paradox

by Heraclitus

ALL politicians are liars, says Mr Waldegrave to the Foreign Affairs Select Committee. Lord Justice Scott then accuses Mr Waldegrave of telling a lie. Mr Waldegrave, who is a politician, replies that he is not a liar. How do we know if he is telling the truth?

Answer on a postcard to Brainteaser, c/o the Cones Charter Hotline, Open Government House, Whiteliehall, London SW1. The sender of the first correct solution opened will receive a deluxe Supergun labelled "Trouser-press".

JUDGE DREDD
The Ultimate Lawman from the year 2000 A.D. (which is when his report is coming out).

AT THE END OF THE 20TH CENTURY, ONLY ONE MAN STOOD AGAINST THE CORRUPT POLITICO-DRONES: JUDGE SCOTT (SURELY DREDD. EDD ?)

I AM THE LAW!

WE DIDN'T KNOW WHAT WE WERE DOING — WE WERE THE GOVERNMENT FOR GOD'S SAKE!

BUT THE JUSTICE MACHINE WAS MERCILESS....

KER-LEAK

THIS REPORT IS ALL LIES!

HOW DO YOU KNOW?

SCOTT REPORT

ER...BECAUSE WE TOLD THEM TO YOU

WITH THEIR BACKS TO THE WALL, THE DRONES FOUGHT BACK

KER-SMEAR

YOU'LL NEVER GET AWAY WITH THIS, SCOTT!

BECAUSE WE WILL!

MORAL: THE LONG ARM OF THE LAW HAS BEEN SOLD TO IRAQ

KHAN/GOLDSMITH WEDDING
EXCLUSIVE PICTURE

Here comes the bride. Fire!

"Hey, wow! Trevor's found a way to trainspot on the Internet"

HURD AND MAJOR

The Final Episode

(Major is playing banjo, and singing "When the Red, Red, Redwood comes Bob-Bob-Bobbing along." He catches fingers in strings which then break).

Major: Yow! This banjo's useless, Hurd.

Hurd: So it would appear, sir, and in that respect it shares much in common with the man playing it.

Major: I say, Hurd, what rot! Things are going dashed well.

Hurd: Indeed sir, I gather you have resigned.

Major: But only so I can get my job back, don't you see? Pretty clever wheeze, eh, Hurd? *You* wouldn't have thought that one up, even after eating all that fish, what?

Hurd: That is sadly correct, sir, and given the situation as it stands I feel the time has come to proffer my *own* resignation.

(Major drops banjo on foot)

Major: Double yow! Leaving? You? Me? What?

Hurd: Touched as I am by your loyalty and concern, sir, I must reassure you that my departure is undertaken entirely for your benefit. I feel I am a burden upon you and things would go much better for you if I were to bow out and make way for a younger man.

Major: I can't believe it, Hurd. Who will clear up all the mess I make?

Hurd: Ah! I have taken the liberty, sir, of arranging for a Mr Rifkind to take over. He is a Scottish gentleman with impeccable credentials.

Major: But hang it! I don't want a chap in a skirt, Hurd, I want you! Talk about rats leaving the sinking ship!! *(Long pause)* Not that it is sinking, mind you.

Hurd: Exactly, sir. And it will not sink a great deal better without me. As the poet puts it, *Ave atque valet.*

Major: And what's that supposed to mean when it's at home?

Hurd: It is Latin, sir. I believe it is roughly translated as "so long, sucker!"

(Hurd exits slamming door. Major picks up bagpipes and begins to play "The Rifkinds are coming awa' awa'". Bagpipes explode)

THE END

CAST IN FULL:

Douglas Hurd . . . . . . **Stephen Fry**

Bertie Major . . . . **Hugh Laurie**

Malcolm Rifkind . **Rab C. Nesbitt**

NEXT WEEK: New series of Poirot returns beginning with "Poirot in Toronto: The Strange Case of Lord Archer and the Missing Suits."

THE ROYAL WEDDING OF THE YEAR

♥ ♥ ♥ ♥ AN EYE SOUVENIR ♥ ♥ ♥ ♥

That's what I call ball-tampering

HOW THEY ARE RELATED

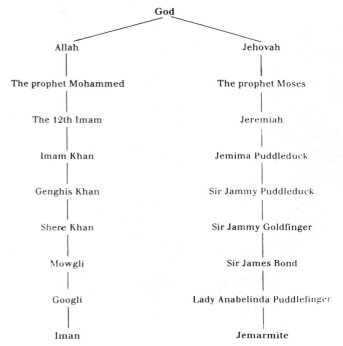

```
                        God
                         |
          ┌──────────────┴──────────────┐
        Allah                         Jehovah
          |                             |
The prophet Mohammed           The prophet Moses
          |                             |
    The 12th Imam                   Jeremiah
          |                             |
      Imam Khan                 Jemima Puddleduck
          |                             |
     Genghis Khan            Sir Jammy Puddleduck
          |                             |
     Shere Khan              Sir Jammy Goldfinger
          |                             |
       Mowgli                    Sir James Bond
          |                             |
       Googli              Lady Anabelinda Puddlefinger
          |                             |
        Iman                       Jemarmite
```

IT WAS the wedding of the century. No one has ever seen anything like it. From every corner of the globe they came — the world's most beautiful people.

Royalty, politics, the arts, showbusiness, sport — they were all represented in the midsummer sunshine outside the Neasden registry office, where the happy couple were married for the first time since last Tuesday.

The roll-call reads like a cross between the Almanac de Gotha, Debrett's and Who's Who all rolled into one.

Among the stars who were present were:

■ **Disgraced former junior minister Mr Anthony Lambton.**

■ **TV presenter Sir David Frost.**

■ **Former top model Jerry Hall.**

■ **Ex-gaolbird Taki "I once played for Greece in the Davis Cup" Takealotofcokeupthenos.**

■ **Er...**

■ **That's it.**

And that was only the cream. Also on the roll of glamour were:

● **Mr John Aspinall, the zoo-owner, accompanied by his third wife Shaka, the killer-chimpanzee.**

● **The late Lord Lucan.**

● **The late Mr George "15 Minutes" Fame.**

● **Top businessman Sir David Frost.**

● **HRH the Princess Michael of Plageria.**

● **Surprisingly few Moslems.**

♥ ♥ ♥ ♥ ♥ ♥ ♥ ♥ ♥ ♥ ♥ ♥

That Sumptuous Goldsmith-Khan Wedding Feast Menu In Full

Fishpaste

— ✳ —

Marmite Sandwiches

— ✳ —

Roast Talbot

— ✳ —

Jam Fingers

— ✳ —

To drink: nothing

♥ ♥ ♥ ♥ ♥ ♥ ♥ ♥ ♥ ♥ ♥ ♥ ♥

YES! IT'S MYSTIC

MAG

The old crone looks into her empty crystal glass and comes up with a load of balls.

looking ahead at what's in store this week.

★ The Portaloo
(29 May–14 December)

Those born under the sign of the Portaloo may have high hopes for a new job but beware! Your star could be eclipsed by someone even more right-wing and unpleasant than you! Best colour is blue.

★ Arsa Major
(23 March–22 March)

Your moon is in the descendent as it has been for some time. Beware of everyone. You should not get up or even get out of bed. You must look forward to a new job, a new house and a new life of obscurity. You must also face the fact that you were a hopeless failure, unlike me.

★ The Hurdsman
(14 July–14 October)

It's time to pack it in and seek pastures new. Your moon is down the toilet, mate. You were never any good anyway with your stupid voice and silly hair. Serves you right for sucking to the Euros. Go on, scram!! Favourite city: Maastricht.

★ The Shepherd
(1 February–2 February)

If you are a shepherd, stay up in the proverbial hills away from the metaphysical wolves. Very few women can make it to the top, only *me* in fact, so sod off you silly old bag.

★ Hezza the Hunter
(30 December–31 February)

Your health is not good and I would not risk it any further. Additional stress such as standing for Leader of the Conservative party will almost certainly kill you — I hope.

★ Red Wood
(Next 100 years)

Tomorrow belongs to you! You must grasp the opportunity while you can. Nail your colours to the mast! Let loose the dogs of war! Go my beauty! Go! Exterminate! Exterminate! Exterminate!

Mystic Mag is unwell and is unable to finish her predictions this week.

"Everything all right?"

BOTT'S CLOSES DOWN AT LAST
No one mourns

by Our Medical Staff **Baillie Vasectomy**

AFTER a prolonged campaign, Britain's least loved medical institution was finally closed down last night.

For centuries St Bottomley's, or Bott's, was known throughout the world for its dedicated lack of care for patients.

Situated in the heart of London, Botts specialised in long, boring speeches, packed with meaningless figures and bureaucratic jargon.

Said one leading surgeon Sir Vical Smear: "It is a national disgrace that they are closing St Bott's now. They should have closed it down years ago."

THE STORY SO FAR: Handsome debonair actor Hugh Grant has been caught having oral sex with a black prostitute. Now read on…

To err is human...

THE glorious summer sunshine shone brilliantly from a clear blue sky, sending a golden glow among the ancient rolling hills of Wiltshire. The sleepy stone cottages of Little Legover basked in the midsummer heat. Bees hummed lazily in the hollyhocks and a thousand long-lens cameras clicked rhythmically from the top of 14-foot ladders.

Every rheumy eye of Fleet Street's finest was focussed on the deeply moving scene being played out below them on the well-manicured lawn of the Old Manor House.

Beneath the timeless mullioned windows, in the shade of a gnarled fellatio tree, a young man held out a plate of salad to the most beautiful woman the world had ever known.

"I can explain everything," he stammered, for the hundredth time, "if only you would listen."

"We *are* listening," came the reply from a hundred voices behind the wall. "Can you speak up a bit?"

"Sorry," said the young man. "I'll take it from the top. Now, where were we? Oh yes — I've been a bloody fool. I don't know what came over me."

"How could you?" she sobbed, as huge translucent tears welled up in her perfectly-formed eyes and gushed unchecked down the exquisite peach-skin purity of her cheeks.

The world-famous heartthrob, whose films had grossed 2000 billion dollars worldwide, put out a hand and made as if to place it consolingly on her swan-white shoulder.

"Take your filthy paws off me," she spat, like an angry lioness, her face contorted into a hideous scar of hatred — hardly recognisable as the pouting beauty whose peerless features had graced every page of the *Daily Telegraph* each morning for the past six months.

"It was a moment of madness," he stammered in explanation. "It was only because I was lonely without you."

"Don't lie to me!" she shrieked. "You can save your lies for the courts."

So saying, she hurled the plate of uneaten salad at his suntanned, finely-chiselled features. A delicate trickle of vinaigrette ran down his Reeves & Mortimer polo shirt and from behind the wall came the raucous laughter of the world's highest-paid journalists. They had got what they had come for.

A STRANGE bearded figure in a low cut dress sat alone in the first-class compartment of the 8.14 to Paddington. In her rococo-patterned Benetton travel bag were just a few hurriedly snatched up keepsakes of the dying embers of their love.

What did they mean now, these tattered clippings, bank statements and old copies of *Hello*?

"Ticket please Miss Hurley." The conductor's voice interrupted her reverie.

"But, how did you know?" she whispered, in a faltering voice.

"It was the beard," replied the kindly official from beneath his Great Western Trains turban. "I've seen it on the TV."

Suddenly the mobile trilled on the seat beside her.

"Excuse me," she said. "It may be the studio."

Cupping the telephone to her immaculate, Dresden-shepherdess-like ear, she murmured "Who is this?"

"It's me."

The manly voice was racked with pain and self-doubt. "I've been thinking it over. Us, I mean."

Her heart beat faster, in time with the thudding of the train wheels as it slowed imperiously to a halt due to signalling problems between Swindon and Didcot Parkway.

"Me too."

"What I mean…" he said.

"Yes?"

"You know, we've got to stay together. For the sake of…"

"Yes, darling?"

"…for the sake of the money".

"Oh darling, I'm so happy. That's what my agent said too."

She slowly put the phone back onto the seat, and the whole world suddenly seemed to be lit by the glow of a thousand rainbows.

From somewhere she seemed to hear a disembodied voice.

"This is your senior conductor speaking. This train has terminated. We advise customers to continue their journey by alternative forms of transport."

NEXT WEEK: But To Forgive Divine.

© S. Krin 1995.

New From Gnome!

THE 1995 TORY LEADERSHIP ELECTION

64-Piece Commemorative Dinner Service

Life-Size

FOR years to come the Gnome Redwood-Major Dinner Set will remain a priceless investment as well as a unique memento of the greatest political event of our time.

Each of the 64 pieces in this priceless collection is handcrafted in bone-china-style unbreakable Scruton, and bears the likeness of the two contenders in the great leadership battle, specially painted by world-famous ceramologist Ralph Stodswell R.A.C.

Each item has been authenticated by leading TV historian Andrew Roberts as having been salvaged from the wreck of the S.S. Toryparty, which sank with all hands in the Year Of Our Lord 1995.

Each set contains the following items:
14 Dinner Plates (212 mm in diameter)
6 Soup Tureens (EC-approved size)
1 Mustard Saucer
12 Dessert Dishes
6 Grapefruit Segment Basins
8 Side-Dishes
12 Milk Pipkins

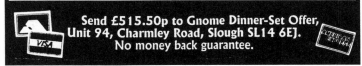

Send £515.50p to Gnome Dinner-Set Offer, Unit 94, Charmley Road, Slough SL14 6EJ. No money back guarantee.

ken

ST CAKE'S BOY BECOMES YOUNGEST EVER CABINET MINISTER

by Our Education And Employment Staff **Conrad Blackboard**

A SIXTH-former at the £41,000-a-term independent school St Cake's was today promoted straight into the Cabinet, becoming the first teenager ever to hold one of the major departments of state.

He is **William Squitt**, 16, who has been appointed to be Secretary of State for Customer Care.

The school's £41,000-a-week headmaster Mr Chenevix-Kipling praised his young pupil, saying: "Squitt is one of our ablest students. He has 7 GCSEs, and has been the Secretary of the school Debating Society for two terms."

Portaloo Sunset

Last term, Squitt proposed the motion: "This house believes that all unemployed people should be sent to prison."

Squitt also published a special edition of the school magazine,

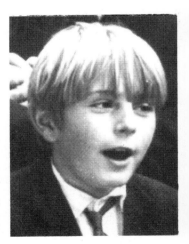

Cakes and Cakemen, arguing that the school should re-introduce capital punishment for drug-takers.

Squitt was a great admirer of Mr Michael Portaloo until last week, and once invited his hero to speak at the school's Mosley Society annual dinner.

SLEAZE LATEST

AITKEN DENIES SEX SMEAR

by Our Filth Correspondent
Janet Street-Walker

FORMER Treasury Minister Jonathan Aitken today denied all knowledge of an alleged 27-month affair with a high-class call girl.

"I may well have attended meetings with this woman," he said, "but at no time did she tell me what she was doing. I was completely in the dark until she turned the lights on".

Super Gun

Mr Aitken claimed that no formal record of the meetings were kept and that he himself had been out of the room when the alleged incidents occurred.

ON OTHER PAGES

BOTTOMLEY TAKES OVER AT HERITAGE

Stonehenge to close p.94

I am resigning to spend more time with my solicitors

"Don't give me that pathetic martyred look, Sebastian"

Poetry Corner

Lines On The Award Of A Knighthood To Sir Clifford Richard

So. Congratulations then
Sir Cliff.
And Celebrations.

Now you are
A walking, talking,
Living Knight.

Soon you will be going on
A Summer Holiday.
No doubt!

Once again we say
Congratulations!

Because I cannot remember
Any more of your hits.

And Keith's Mum
Is in hospital.

Glenda Thribb (© All newspapers)

Advertisement

New from Gnome!

JONAH LOMU Paperclips

At last — the ultimate way to tackle those stationery problems!

As used* by Rugby's new superstar — the man they are calling the human try-machine.

Trample through your paperwork, ride roughshod through your desk melee, break through to office success!

Yes, you'll score every time with Gnome Jonah Lomu paperclips.

*probably

 ✳ Comes in giant size pack of 1000
Colours: ● All-Black *(not available)*
● Silver *(£445.99 + VAT)*

Apply to GNOME LOMU OFFER (formerly Gnome Rob Andrew Offer), Unit 147b, The Trading Estate, Crawley

The Night I Knew It Would All Go Wrong

by Britain's Top Dramatist SIMON GRAY

*Extracts from his forthcoming book
The Whingeing Playwright.*

CHAPTER 94

I AM horribly let down at a preview at the Swindon Hexagon. Half-way through Act II of my brilliant new play, *Cell Out* (based on the historic meeting in prison of Nelson Mandela and Gerry Adams), the scenery collapsed and the bars of the prison windows suddenly fell on to the stage! Adams and Mandela, played by Stephen Fry and Frank Bruno, looked at each other in silence.

Then Stephen (Adams), instead of continuing with his explanation of how there was no possibility of escape and that this imprisonment was a metaphor for the whole of the country, suddenly came out of character, picked up the bars and said "Look at these complete bar-stewards."

The audience erupted in gales of laughter, destroying the tension that had built up during a beautifully crafted and intensely moving two-hour scene which had linked the plight of Northern Ireland and South Africa in an extraordinarily clever fashion.

Frank Bruno, to his credit, stayed in character and desperately tried to get the scene back on course.

"I'm ducking and diving. You know what I mean, Gerry," he ad-libbed.

But it was too late. By then Stephen had messed it all up and ruined everything. And worse was to come.

At the Dame Ian McKellen Theatre in Leatherhead only a week later (where, incidentally, we had opened to rave reviews in the *Leatherhead Examiner*), Frank's trousers inexplicably fell down just at the point where Mandela was holding up his ball and chain and explaining that the ball was a metaphor for the world.

The pathetic Stephen of course could not resist the chance to ingratiate himself with the audience and joked: "How fitting, given that this play is a lot of balls." Once again the spell was broken. My brilliant play was forgotten and the audience were reduced to laughter, cheers and cries of: "Thank God, good old Stephen has saved the whole evening!"

NEXT WEEK: Stephen ruins the West End opening by not sending me a card and not giving Frank a big, big hug.

© *LuvvieTrash in cooperation with The Whingeing Playwright 1995.*

FRY'S E-MAIL MESSAGE TO GRAY THAT SAID IT ALL

Sorry. Sorry. Sorry. Sorry. I'm off to Bruges. God bless and get stuffed.

YOUNG JONATHAN AITKEN

"At the time of my client's denial, he understood you to be referring to another cherry tree which he had in fact not chopped down"

GRAND EYE COMPETITION

NOW IT COULD BE YOU TO NAME GAZZA'S LOVECHILD!

Study the names below and tick the one of your choice:

- ☐ Bazza
- ☐ Gizza
- ☐ Hezza
- ☐ Pizza
- ☐ Rozzer
- ☐ Dominic Lawson

Whichever name wins most support from Eye readers will automatically be given to Gazza's toddler!

THE TIMES SEPTEMBER 1 1939

Time To Do Nothing

by Simon Jenkins, Alan Clark, Ann Leslie and others.

THOSE of us who really understand the situation in Eastern Europe know that there is only one sensible course of action for Britain to adopt in this lamentable crisis.

Just because we have all been reading stories of atrocities and supposedly innocent civilians being ethnically cleansed, the more excitable commentators have been clamouring for military action against Herr Hitler.

But anyone who understands the logic of realpolitik as we do would know that this is just hysterical knee-jerk wishful thinking.

Do we really want young British lives sacrificed in a foreign quarrel?

Poland is a far-away country in which we British have no strategic or any other interest. What the Germans and the Poles choose to do to each other in the heat of war is entirely their own business. We should let them get on with it. Yes, there will be casualties, but they will not be British.

If the sentimental, whingeing interventionists get their way, all informed opinion (ie us) agrees that Britain could easily get drawn into a war which could go on for years. It could even escalate into a world-wide conflagration.

No, it is time for wiser counsel to prevail. We must recognise that Herr Hitler and his plans for a Greater Germany are a fact of life. If we really desire peace, it is vital that we should keep out of this mess completely. We must do nothing and do it now.

NURSERY TIMES

FRIDAY, JULY 28 1995

RAPID REACTION FORCE READY TO GO

by Our UN correspondent Christopher Gunless

The Grand Old Duke of York's regiment, consisting of ten thousand men, was on standby last night for immediate despatch up the hill.

"What I am to do," said commander the Grand Old Duke, "is to march my men straight up to the top of the hill and then withdraw as fast as is humanly possible.

"I don't want to get bogged down at the top of the hill and my main priority is not to lose any men when I'm up there.

"But rest assured," he continued. "This will send a clear message to the world. That when we're up we are up. And when we are down we are down. And when we are only half-way up, we are fulfilling the UN mandate exactly."

═══ On Other Pages ═══

All King's Horses and Men Powerless To Assist Wounded Humpty

'Beyond our brief,' says General

"So what else do you hypnotise apart from rabbits?"

THE FATTY LAWSON DIET

I lost millions of pounds for everyone in the country

Notes & Queries

A service by our readers for our readers (as seen in all other newspapers)

QUESTION: Could you please tell us what the American army is for, if it is not allowed to fight? — *Mrs Ethel Rusbridger, Canary Wharf.*

□ THE American army is an organisation set up to enable members of the gay and lesbian community to exercise their rights by joining it. It also provides an equal-opportunity framework for women to participate in command situations which do not involve combat. — *General P.C. Dolittle III Jnr.*

QUESTION: Does anyone know why the British army has to ask the Americans for helicopters, since we have already spent billions of pounds buying helicopters from them in the first place? — *M. Heseltine, 10a Downing Street. Deputy Prime Minister and First Lord of the Jungle.*

□ READER Heseltine is quite right to say that we have spent billions of pounds on buying US helicopter stock, but there is a snag. They are the wrong sort of helicopters for dealing with the hilly terrain of the former Yugoslavia. This means that we have to ask for American helicopters, which we know they are not going to give us, so that we have yet another excuse for doing nothing. — *Brig. Trumper-Smythe.*

ANSWERS TO PREVIOUS QUESTIONS: It is quite wrong for Professor Norman Stone to claim that the reason Fox's Glacier Mints have a picture of a polar bear and not a fox on the wrapping is because they were previously known as Bear's Glacier Mints. The explanation is quite simple. The artist, commissioned by Mr Ezekiel Fox (1858-1907) to design the original wrapper, was an Eskimo artist, Mr Mahood, who had never seen a fox. In the Inuit language all four-legged creatures are designated by the same word, which means "bear". Hence the charming drawing with which generations of mint-lovers have become familiar. — *Alan Sweetpaper, Editor, Mints and Mintmen, London EC1*

ANSWERS PLEASE: Is it true that frogs can jump backwards? Is there such a thing as a left-handed spoon? Is it true that the EC have regulated the size of toilet tissue? Who writes Jeffrey Archer's books? Why does the *Eye* keep printing that unfunny picture of Andrew Neill and the Asian girl?

ATTROCIOUS

TACKI
(The World's 2nd Worst Columnist)

Incredibly

LORD WHITE is a thoroughly good egg. He is very rich. So is Lord Hanson. I like them both very much indeed.

Thin

LORD JENKINS is a social climber and a snob. He is also middle-class. And not very rich. I really don't like him. All he does is suck up to the upper classes.

Stuff

MY OLD friend Lord Ipswich is terrifically rich. Yesterday he took me for a ride in his private jet. We flew all the way to Gstaad where we met the following rich people: Jimmy Goldsmith, Lord White, Lord Hanson and Lord Ipswich. I like them all very much.

NEXT WEEK: Taki meets some more rich people and names them in his column.

GNOME LEISURE INC
(Slags 'R' Us)

MAKE YOUR OWN
PAULA YATES™

All the fun of the cosmetic surgeon in your own front room!
Paula is just waiting for you to turn her from a plain middle-aged housewife into a dazzling superbabe as seen in *Hello!*
Simply cut out the accessories and stick them on with superglue! It's what she did!!

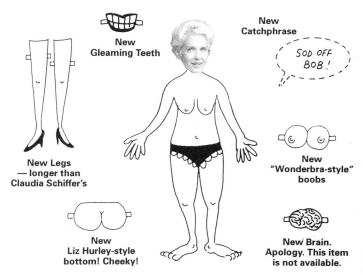

New Gleaming Teeth

New Catchphrase

SOD OFF BOB!

New Legs — longer than Claudia Schiffer's

New "Wonderbra-style" boobs

New Liz Hurley-style bottom! Cheeky!

New Brain. Apology. This item is not available.

THOSE LABOUR LANDSLIDES

1945

We're going to have a new world

1964

We're going to have a new Britain

1997

We're going to have... er... a new Government

The Cheshire Cat explained to Alice that he was a great admirer of Tony Blair

BLAIR-MURDOCH SUMMIT
That Speech In Full

Blair: Ladies and gentlemen and Your Holiness The Supreme Ruler of Sun and Sky Rupertus Murdochus Maximus, King of Kings, Timeslord of all you survey. Greetings from the planet England.

Murdochus: Greetings, Pommy Weakling. Get on with it. You've got two minutes.

Blair: I come in suppliance. Not to beg for your support at the next election. Oh no. We speak as equals. I as the leader of the New Labour Party. And you as Supreme Ruler of the Universe, Grand Controller of all known media that are in the earth or beyond it.

Murdochus: I said get on with it, creep.

Blair: You and I, O Great One, have much in common. We are both admirers of Mrs Thatcher. We both believe in the free market. We are both opposed to the trade unions. We both favour a grant-maintained independent sector in education. We are both devout Christians. And so on. We are the radicals now. And if we win the election, as with your help I know we shall, we shall radically do nothing at all to interfere with your inalienable right to own as many newspapers and TV stations, both satellite and terrestrial, as you want.

Murdochus: Here is the cheque for your expenses.

Blair: Oh thank you, thank you, most munificent of princes.

Murdochus: Time's up. Throw him out.

The Alternative Rocky Horror Service Book

No. 94. A Service of Reconciliation To Mark The 50th Anniversary Of The Allied War Crimes At Hiroshima And Nagasaki.

The President (of the Phuwotascorcha Corporation, Tokyo, new owners of Westminster Abbey): Welcome, honoured guests, to this Peace Ceremony to mark Britain's repentance for its past in the unforgivable act of genocide perpetrated against the innocent people of Imperial Japan in 1945.

All: Ah, so.

The President: I shall now ask the Archbishop of Canterbury to offer a formal apology for British war crimes.

Dr Carey-Flannel: You know... in a very real sense... war terrible business... faults on both sides.

The President (voice rising to a scream): No, Archbishop. Fault on one side only.

Carey: Alright, have it your own way, since you own the building.

The Choir shall then whistle the anthem "Col. Bogey" from the film The Bridge Over The River Kwai (new version showing how British prisoners tortured their Japanese captors by dying in their thousands of starvation).

The Dismissal

The President: Sayonara, English johnnies. For you the service is over.

All leave

The Daily Telegraph

FINAL

35p

FRIDAY, AUGUST 11, 1995

Good News For Tories

Record Temperatures Boost Major's Election Hopes

By Our Political Staff Hugh Wotascorcher

AT LAST it's good news for the Tories!

As Britain sweltered in the greatest heatwave since records were kept, top government sources were convinced that the elusive "feelgood factor" had at last returned.

As supermarket check-out girl Sharon Waterhouse, 19, stripped to her undies and dived into the Serpentine, she said: "It's fantastic! Who wants Benidorm when you've got Tory weather like this?"

From Berwick to Biggleswade, from Cockermouth to Kircudbright, from *(Get on with it. Ed)*, the story was the same.

Old age pensioners danced in fountains, toddlers played happily in tropical-style sunshine, and Britain's Mr Whippys clocked up record sales.

Major-ca

No wonder flights were diverted from Hawaii and Florida to Tory Gatwick and Edward Heath-row.

Make no mistake! Britain's weather is leading the world!

As one top Tory put it: "We have put in the groundwork for this weather over the last 16 years — and now at least we are reaping the benefits.

"And all thanks to John Major and his new Cabinet team, under Mr Heseltine."

Clean Blair Act

However, the Opposition were quick to point out that the Tories have got it wrong again about the weather.

"What we want is sensible New Labour rain," said a front bench spokesman. "Only Tony Blair and New Labour can produce the sort of drizzle that can make Britain wet again."

The New Lib Dems under Paddy Ashdown said that both the old new parties had got it wrong.

"What Britain needs is not sunshine or rain," said Mr Splashdown. "What we need is the unique combination of fog and mist which only the new Dem Libs can provide."

Tory Test Triumph

By Our Political Staff Will Len Hutton

TORY election hopes soared yesterday when England won yet another Test Match.

Mike Atherton's men trounced the West Indies with a stunning display of Tory bowling and Conservative batting.

Said a source close to Number 10: "We have put in the groundwork for this victory for ten years and at last we are reaping the reward."

Liz and Hugh Together Again – Thanks to Major

'Rift Healed'

By Our Political Staff Simon Hefferniceday

THE DISUNITY which has plagued the country ever since the sleaze factor hit Hugh Grant has at last come to an end.

Thanks to Mr Major's election victory over John Redwood, Hugh and girlfriend Liz Hurley (see pics pp 7-14) have decided to "stay together" until the next general election.

Said one top Tory source: "I think this has to be seen as a personal triumph for John. We have been laying the ground for this for the last 16 years, and now at last we are reaping the rewards."

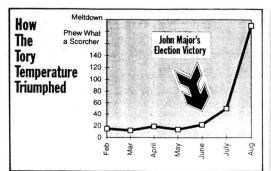

How The Tory Temperature Triumphed

Meltdown
Phew What a Scorcher
John Major's Election Victory
140
120
100
80
60
40
20
0
Feb Mar April May June July Aug

INSIDE ☐ M25 on fire as hundreds flee melting tar horror 3 ☐ Heatcrazed ants attack toddler 4 ☐ Car fumes will kill millions says Gummer 7 ☐ Why oh why is it so hot? asks red-faced lunatic Paul Johnson 8 ☐ Why women should take all their clothes off in the heat, by Dr Le Fanu (plus loads of pics) 9 ☐ Prom audience suffocates to death in Mahler agony 10

Plus Special Readers' Offer

The Daily Telegraph 'Outback' Hat. The battery-powered Panama-style hat with internal fan will keep you cool in tropical Britain. Ideal for Glyndebourne, Garsington, Goodwood or the Garrick.

WITH KIDS IN MIND

An Eye Annual Cut Out 'n' Keep School Holiday Special

7 Aug. Lincoln's Inn Fields. All Day. Slovenian Puppet Theatre. Famous folk tales acted out by graduates of the renowned Zibgob Academy. Stories include "Misolovsha and the Bear", "The Great Castle of Blomsk" and "The Tragic Tale of Irma Kurtz". **Age 3-7.** *Admission free.*

9 Aug. Yeovil Castle. Re-creation of the Civil War Battle of Barriemoor (1644) by members of the East Somerset Fire Brigade. Authentic costumes and taped sound effects. 2 performances hourly. **Age 12 onwards.** *Admission £17.50.*

15 Aug. Douglas Town Hall, Isle of Man. Exhibition of traditional Celtic Harps and Flutes. Workshops with master instrument makers and special evening concert by Siobahn Doing and Finbarr Boing. **Age 15+.** *Admission 5p (4p unwaged).*

23 Aug. Insect-o-Rama, Nottingham. New educational theme park with thrilling Ant-Rides and Underwater Spider Experience. **Age 2+.** *Admission £25 per car.*

31 Aug. Tate Gallery, Liverpool. All Day. Junior Turner Prize. Kids are invited to do whatever they like in a mixed media environment and create their own masterpieces. **Age Under 5.** *Admission: Free. £25,000 to winner.* (Judges: Maggie Hambling, George Melly and Joanna Lumley.)

All Sept. McDonalds. Take your children out for a MacHoliday Treat (MacBurger, MacFries, MacShake, MacIndigestion). All for under £3.99. *(That's quite enough. Ed.)*

Peter McKay's Top Ten Tips for Keeping Cool in the Heatwave

1. Wrap up warm.
2. Close all windows and doors.
3. Turn on central heating.
4. Drink plenty of hot soup.
5. Wear extra socks in bed.
6. Stay indoors at all times.
7. Er…
8. Isn't life grandy?
9. And dandy??
10. That's it.

© *The World's Worst Columnist*

CARRY ON PSEUD!

THE NEW Carry On film set in a Media Studies Department where the staff are earnestly analysing the role of the Carry On genre in British cinematography.

Starring **Kenneth Williams** as Professor Ivor Thesis, **Sid James** as Professor Arty Farty and **Barbara Windsor** as the gorgeous Dee Construction.

(Silly music. Dee enters with her PhD in her hand)

Thesis: Blimey, that's a big one!

Dee: Cheeky!

Thesis: Research paper on a post-modern approach to Carry On films, I meant!

Dee: I've come to give it to you.

Farty: I'd like to give it to you!!

Dee: Ooh-er!

Thesis: We're reconsidering the whole Carry On *oeuvre* as a sort of self-referential statement of high camp. Because let's face it, the films have had their knockers!

Dee: Cheeky!

Farty: We're going to get to the bottom of their lasting appeal.

Dee: Ooh-er!

Thesis: Irony! Irony! They've all got irony!

Farty: As comedy, I think it stands up pretty well.

Thesis: I wish mine did!

Dee: Cheeky!

Farty: That's the crux of it!

Dee: Ooh-er!

Thesis: It's exactly what my piece said in the *Guardian.*

Farty: Was it a big one?

Dee: Cheeky!

Thesis: No, I did a very good job.

Farty *(holding nose):* Crikey! I hope you opened the window!

Dee: Ooh-er!

(Continues for several hours)

A Chief Commissioner writes

In the absence of the cabdriver on holiday we have invited **Sir Paul Condon**, the Chief Commissioner of the Metropolitan Police, to write on an issue of topical importance.

■ I mean, I'm no racist, right guv, but the facts speak for themselves which is that 98% of muggings in London are done by the darkies. Let's not beat about the bush. It can't carry on like this. D'you know what I'd do about these muggers and I'm serious? I'd go up to that Bernie Grant and the rest of the community leaders and I'd say "Why can't you do something to get it sorted?" I had that John Fashanu in the back of my station the other day...

Some of them have got criminal records this long

Luckily for the Pied Piper, all the Hamelin rats belonged to the Orange Order

DRINK YOUR OWN URINE
Gummer's Shock Plea

by Our Water Staff
Hugh Water-Scorcher

ENVIRONMENT minister John Gummer yesterday praised Britain's water companies for their "superb management" of water supplies in the current drought.

"The newly privatised companies," said Mr Gumboot, "have achieved all that we could have hoped for. They have managed to sell all their water, and it's still only August!"

Gummer Time And The Lying Is Easy

Standing in an empty reservoir near his East Anglia home, Mr Gummer lashed out at "greedy" water customers, who "took all there was and still wanted more".

Said the angry minister: "These people never know when to stop. They think that water is just something that comes out of a tap.

"If these waterhogs want unlimited supplies they should provide the water themselves from their own resources."

Mr Gummer stressed that, so long as it complied with EU quality standards, urine was "ideal" for the following purposes:

● **drinking**
● **washing the car**
● **watering the marrows**
● **boiling rice**

Daily Mail

NEWSPAPER OF THE YEAR 35p

FRIDAY, AUGUST 25, 1995

IS THIS THE END FOR BLAIR?

Labour Revolt Grows

By Our Political Staff A. Liar

LABOUR leader Tony Blair was last night reeling under yet another savage assault from his own party, prompting Westminster insiders to predict that he will be lucky to win a single seat at the next election. *(This is good stuff — Lord Rothermere, prop.)*

The latest blow to Blair's tottering leadership came in a blistering broadside from a highly-respected West Midlands councillor, Ron Grobb, interviewed on the influential radio programme *Good Morning Stoke-on-Trent.*

Speaking to DJ Kevin Snazz, Mr Grobb, 57, said: "Sometimes I wonder whether Tony Blair really knows what's going on in Stoke-on-Trent."

Vote Conservative

Mr Grobb's astonishing outburst follows a series of hammerblows which have left Blair dazed and on the ropes, waiting only for the final knockout which will be delivered by John Major at the next election. *(Brilliant. Take a pay rise — Lord R.)*

This is the amazing sequence of events which have made the past fortnight "The Ten Days That Shook Blair's World" and left him reeling against the ropes *(We've had that — pay rise withdrawn. LR.)*

● **August 1.** *Daily Mail* reveals that Labour elder statesman Roy Hattersley doesn't like Tony Blair very much.

● **August 3.** Leading Labour backbencher Eric Spittle, MP for Dunwoody East, writes in the widely-read journal of the Firefighter's Union *Fires and Firemen*: "It could be argued that the centralising tendency in Blair's strategy will prove counter-productive in some circumstances."

● **August 10.** *Daily Mail* reveals that top Blair aide Peter Moustache spent his holiday in the nobs' paradise of Tuscany.

● **An** independent poll commissioned by the *Daily Mail* reveals that a staggering 100% of people in the offices of Associated Newspapers think that Blair is "finished as a political force" and that he should "resign at once".

● **Er...**

● **Ron Grobb, a rising star in** West Midlands local government circles, attacks Blair for being out of touch with the grass roots.

Don't Vote Labour

Make no mistake — the so-called Blair honeymoon is dead and buried.

The Labour Party is exposed for what it has always been — a group of loony leftists feuding amongst themselves while the Conservative government gets on with the job of giving this country the kind of leadership it deserves.

INSIDE: 'I Agree That Labour Is Hopeless Now That I'm Not In It Any More Either' by Gerald Kaufman 8, 'It's Too Hot And Blair's To Blame, says Britain's Voice Of Controversy B. Pad 11, Unfunny Blair cartoon by Mac 42

Extracts from the SCOTT DIARY

The Final Hours of a Very Gallant English Gentleman

August 1st

OH GOD! This is an impossible task. We are already eight months overdue and still there is no end in sight. Today another 300 pages from Waldegrave nearly buried us, but somehow we kept going.

August 4th

POOR Presiley Baxendale! It has been too much for her. I think the Howe Paper Mountain will finish her off. She has had no sleep now for three months. Always reading, reading, reading…

August 9th

ANOTHER impasse! The Attorney General is blocking our way with over 500 pages of objections. Can we find a way around? I should never have taken on this job. I wanted to serve my country, do something to make Britain proud again.

But we are forgotten. Snowed in by a Whitehall blizzard.

August 12th

BAXENDALE walked out of the office today saying she could be gone for some time. This leaves me all alone. Oh God…

Here the writing trails away and only a few words can be deciphered. Bastard… Waldegrave… Supergun… Alan Clark… Thatcher…

Scott was discovered underneath an 800ft avalanche of memoranda. He never did reach his goal of producing a report on the Arms to Iraq affair.

IAN BAKER

"Are you saying I can't provide for my kids?"

The Eye Focuses On The Burning Literary Issue Of The Moment

Reprinted from the Times Literary Supplement (shurely 'the Sun'? — Ed)

10 TELL TALE SIGNS WHICH PROVE THAT JANE AUSTEN WAS GAY

1. She was a woman.
2. She was unmarried.
3. She wrote under a man's name (*No she didn't — that was T.S. Eliot. Ed*).
4. She slept in the same bed as her sister.
5. Her sister slept in the same bed as her.
6. She wrote a lot of books, just like Jeanette Winterson.
7. Austen is a well known man's name.
8. She looks like one of them.
9. Er…
10. That's it.

And if you still don't believe us, just look at the titles of her books:
Gay Pride and Prejudice
Of That Persuasion
My Naughty Lesbos Nights With Julie Burchill (*surely 'Sense and Sensibility'? Ed*)

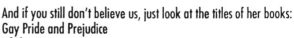

WAS JANE GAY?
Call Jeremy Paxman now on
01-2485-612411
Remember — YOU DECIDE

That Japanese PM's 謝 Apology In Full 罪

AT A certain period in Japanese history (which is not taught in schools due to lack of time in the curriculum) certain unfortunate events took place which so far as the Japanese people were concerned were in a mistaken direction, leading to regrettable consequences which particularly affected our fellow Asians and which, in the light of history (sadly not taught in Japanese schools owing to a shortage of textbooks) may now be regarded as not the kind of thing which we would wish to happen again, constituting as they do a continuing cause of misunderstanding amongst our European friends, especially those who were our guests at the relevant period, those, that is, who are still alive, and *(continued for 94 pages)*.

THE SUN SAYS

THERE is only one apology our boys will accept from the Japs.

That is the mass hari-kiri of every Japanese male over 50.

So hari up, Nips. And our readers will supply the swords.

Send your money now to SUN Send-A-Sword and we'll provide the Nips with the ideal way to celebrate VJ Day.

Tick the box to show where you want Johnny Jap to stick his Sun sword:

☐ **In his belly**

☐ **Down his throat**

☐ **Up his bum**

"Hey — aren't you the frog formerly known as Prince?"

Kerber

PHILIP LARKINTINO

THEY FUCK YOU UP, YOUR MUM AND DAD...

Fantoni

How I'm Going To Change Britain

Redwood's 5-Point Plan
(produced in association with the John Redwood Foundation For Advanced Conservative Philosophy)

1. Single mothers? String 'em up.

2. How to slash billions off the budget? Shoot the unemployed.

3. Europe? Sod off, Delors.

4. Queen Mother — don'tcha love her?

5. Law and order. String 'em all up.

6. John Major — aren'tcha sick of him?

© J. Redwood, Fellow of All Souls (Cab No. 1815)

A SILVIE KRIN SPECIAL
DIANA – Hunter of Men

THE white-tiled walls of the shower room echoed to the lusty refrain of fifteen full-throated English rugby internationals.

"I love a dumb blonde,
A girl who's not too clever.
And I'm going to show her
The biggest tackle ever."

Will Carling, the handsome England captain, soaped his well-built figure, threw back his head and laughed aloud.

This was the life he knew and loved — to be with the lads after a hard training session. The camaraderie, the male-bonding, the sense of well-being.

Not yet thirty, he felt at the peak of physical fitness. He towelled himself dry and splashed his torso liberally with pine-scented "Gazza Pour Homme". He flexed his muscles and took a good look in the mirror. No wonder the world's most beautiful woman had rung him 32 times that morning.

And that would probably be her again now on the mobile phone.

"In the shower, eh? I like the sound of that," purred the familiar voice of the Princess of Wales.

"Well, just out of the shower actually. I've got a towel round me." He looked nervously over his shoulder, but his team-mates were still preoccupied trying to push the new prop forward head-first down the toilet.

"Can you talk, Scrummy-Bummy?" she asked.

"Yah. Sure. I'm not at home or anything."

There was a slight pause, and then Diana asked coyly: "And what about *my* nickname — or have you forgotten?"

The muscled sportsman crouched defensively behind his locker door and whispered: "Er... Yummy-Tummy."

"Say it louder," she ordered in that half-joking, half-flirting, half-imperious

(That's enough 'halfs'. Ed) way that was hers and hers alone. It was as if a bolt of lightning had charged down his spine.

"Yummy-Tummy," he repeated.

"Even louder!" she commanded.

"YUMMY-TUMMY!" he yelled, his voice cracking with a mixture of desire and longing.

The room was suddenly quiet and the captain realised that his colleagues had stopped their horseplay and were all staring at him with wide grins spread across their rugged features.

As he tried to hide the phone, they all began to josh him, repeating the words "Yummy Tummy" in silly braying voices.

Then, unbidden, at the back a deep baritone began a chorus which was taken up by the whole team as they ceremoniously carried Carling naked into the car park and locked him out:

"Swing low! Sweet Will-i-a-am,
Comin' for to carry Di home..."

AT LAST! I'm glad you finally made it." The tall svelte woman in the low-cut black Hirohito designer mini-dress left a pregnant pause. "Make yourself comfortable."

Carling sat down on the purple velvet chaise-longue as bidden and looked around the opulent Knopfler Suite at Kensington Palace. On the walls were framed photographs of young men he vaguely recognised carrying mobile phones. Each bore a signature followed by kisses. What was that one? Squidgy... Mr Floppy... Ovalteeny-Weeny...

The Princess of Wales sat down next to him and placed her hand on his well-proportioned thigh.

"My goodness!" she said, batting her immaculate eyelids. "You *are* fit, aren't you?"

Carling coughed. "Well, you know, I... er... work out down the club and all that stuff."

Diana smiled knowingly. "And do you do any other sort of exercise?" There was a long and intimate silence and the lights seemed to be dimming.

"Well, my wife and I quite often go for walks with the dog, you know…"

"Oh yes. Your wife. I don't think we want to talk about her, do we… Scrummy-Bummy?"

"SCRUMMY-BUMMY, eh!" The England rugby hero's wife held up a copy of the *News of the World.* "So *this* is the sort of training you get up to, is it?"

She threw the paper on the floor and before he could muster a defence continued: "Well, let me tell you, Scummy-Dummy, if you so much as *talk* to that woman again you are dead. Do you understand?"

Carling stood cowering before this relentless tirade and wished with his heart that he was facing not the diminutive figure of his petite wife but a hundred Jonah Lomus running at him at the speed of an express train.

Suddenly his world had collapsed. From being the man who had it all, he now felt little more than a chastened child barely able to even splutter an apology for the stolen apple found in his blazer pocket.

"I was just naive," he found himself saying. "I didn't realise… I… I…"

The phone on the table next to the trophy cabinet began to ring, cutting him short. He and his wife both stared at it, their reflections in the cabinet's glass staring back at them in sullen judgement.

"Let it ring," Mrs Carling ordered as his hand moved instinctively towards it. Two more rings. Then the phone stopped and the answering machine took over.

"Hello. This is Julia Carling. Neither Will or I are here to take your call right now. If it's about business, please ring the office on 0171-673 7557. If it's you, you miserable bitch, stay away from my husband or you'll be posing for *Hello!* with no teeth. Understand? Thank you for calling. Please speak after the tone."

But no one spoke. The phone clicked and the line went dead. In the depths of Kensington Palace a blonde woman picked up a rugby ball and threw it as hard as she could at a 17th century Louis Armstrong Mirroir. The glass shattered, like so many of her dreams, into a thousand useless pieces.

(To be continued)

SILLY SEASON SPECIAL

IS BARRYMORE FUNNY?

An *Eye* Probe

Friends of TV's Michael Barrymore have always claimed in private that the top star is "funny". He has been seen telling jokes and consorting with well-known comedians. But the *Eye* can reveal exclusively that behind the public facade of a drunken homosexual, Barrymore is an entirely straight man who has never been able to make jokes with (cont. p. 94)

"Gentlemen, The Queen…"

Who are they – the evil men who will run Britain when Blair seizes power?

by Seamus Spart

WHO are they, the unelected backroom spin doctors who will be manipulating the puppet Blair when he stages his coup d'etat at the next election?

We don't know, but we've made this up to help John Major win the next election.

PHILIP GOULD-BLEND, 27, deeply sinister backstairs guru who once met President Clinton. His clients include Winnie Mandela, Walsall Borough Council and Tetley's Round Tea Bags. Half of so-called "Gould-Blend couple", being married to millionaire publisher and socialist Hurricana Bebop.

ALISTAIR CAMPBELL-SOUP, 21, deeply sinister former columnist on the KGB mouthpiece *Today* newspaper. Convinced a whole generation of political reporters that Neil Kinnock was a genius. Now believes Tony Blair is a genius. Coined election-winning slogan "Forward with New Labour" in 1983.

FELIX MENDELSSOHN, 17, deeply sinister behind-the-scenes composer *(No. Try again. Ed)*.

PETER MANDELASON, 23, deeply sinister behind-the-scenes bachelor and Stalinist. Inventor of the notorious "Red Rose" campaign which won Labour the 1987 election. Designer of Blair's smile, and man who coined the brilliant new slogan "Vote Labour".

TONY BLAIR, 41, deeply sinister and totally unelected leader of tightly-knit group of politically correct persons who have taken over the Labour Party, with the secret agenda of winning the next election. Married to Hillary Clinton Mandela. Deeply sinister. *(I think we've got the point. Ed.)*